THE ART OF OBEDIENCE

10 BIBLICAL FINANCIAL PRINCIPLES TO CHANGE YOUR LIFE

DELORES MCKENZIE

Endorsements

Delores' passion bleeds through these pages. She dares to take God at his Word, and of course God delivers. Then Delores shows us readers the principles she discovered in her time with the Lord.

—Kary Oberbrunner, Author of *Day Job to Dream Job*, *The Deeper Path*, and *Your Secret Name*

Delores' experience and sage advice continue to light a pathway with regard to financial enlightenment and independence to all comers. This book is time well invested!!!

—Dr. Chad G. Ball, MD, MSC, FACS, FRCSC, Associate Professor, University of Calgary.

DEDICATION

To my husband and my children…
To my many mentors and friends,
Thank you for everything.

Congratulations for choosing to take this incredible step toward your financial freedom. As you commence this journey, may this be the transcending light that helps to transform your world into one of an abundant blessing!

THE ART OF OBEDIENCE

What is Obedience?

Obedience is defined as: compliance to the plan; conformity to the pattern; observance of the rules; adherence to the standard; and submission to another's will.

"For as by one man's disobedience many were made sinners, so by the obedience of One shall many be made righteous." (Romans 5:19)

Honor the LORD with thy substance,
and with the first fruits of all thine increase: **Proverbs 3:9-10**

CONTENTS

FOREWORD

Are you Ready to Break Out and Break Free?

Delores' passion bleeds through these pages. She dares to take God at his Word, and of course God delivers. Then Delores shows us readers the principles she discovered in her time with the Lord.

Many people today are imprisoned by debt, fear, and the reality of living paycheck to paycheck. But there is another way and another world. The real question remains, are you willing to explore it?

Through her unique journey, Delores McKenzie has uncovered the power of exercising her faith through true obedience.

She relied upon God's power to break free from the chains of financial bondage and live an optimal life of wellness.

Through *The Art of Obedience* you'll discover 10 Biblical Financial Principles to change your life.

Kary Oberbrunner

CEO of Redeem the Day and Igniting Souls. Co-creator of Author Academy Elite.

Author of *Day Job to Dream Job, The Deeper Path*, and *Your Secret Name*

THE PREMISE

The Art of Obedience explores 10 biblical financial principles that can take you from where you are and lead you to enjoy success in many areas of your life. The author Delores McKenzie believes that obedience to godly principles is a catalyst to having an extraordinary life. Most people live paycheck to paycheck with an endless cycle of debt. This book will help you to understand that your financial health is important to God. It will show you how to live a debt-free life while harnessing the power of His promises through the blessings of giving and exercising your faith through adhering to His will, and be led to a life of true fulfillment. Delores believes true obedience to God is the key to mastering your success.

She would like to take the opportunity to thank you, the reader, for reading this book. It is her intention to help you shape your financial future. This book could literally save the future of families for a few generations. You are encouraged not only to read this information but to apply the principles entwined within the pages of this book just as if you were reaching into the mirror and creating the reflection you truly desire.

The 10 biblical financial principles outlined in this book will help you harness your faith and the power to live a life of optimum financial health. In her walk, Delores has seen many families suffer financially from the pangs of debt, lack of savings, and mostly from lack of knowledge in money management. It is her passion to share information that could break the cycle of poverty for generations to come. Live on less than you make, save and invest the difference, and give to enhance the lives of others.

SPECIAL NOTE TO THE READER

This book is for everyone, but special emphasis is placed on you who are young, you who are in the prime of your life, and you who are going through the fear of retiring and outliving your money. It will show you how to start saving now and create changes in your life that you could never have even imagined. Starting early is good but starting now is the best thing to do in order to avoid the mistakes of others that have gone before you. This book is meant to help you realize your true purpose on earth and the life you were meant to live. God created man in his own image for the main purpose of worshiping him. He has also provided for your wellbeing in many different areas—the physical, emotional, spiritual and by no means least, the financial. As manager and steward of the gifts you have received from God, you will see that as you examine these 10 biblical principles and apply them to your life, you will be led to live an extraordinary life. 1 Corinthians 4:1-2 states, "Let a man so account of us, as of the ministers of Christ, and stewards of the mysteries of God. Moreover, it is required in stewards that a man be found faithful." This faith will lead you to true obedience, and in obedience you will lead a prosperous life. Prosperity is having what you want when you need it, having the freedom to choose, and having enough to be able to do God's will in your life. You may have had an abundant life, but for some reason your financial state has declined. Whether due to a market downturn or mistakes you have made, having financial reverses will not bring one to the end of the world. Instead, this can push you to a new beginning as you take action on the road to financial wellness. God has already paid the ultimate price and His promise is sure. My God makes all grace abound toward you in every favor and earthly blessing, so that you have all sufficiency for all things and will abound to every good work.

I pray that as you read this book your faith in God will be increased and you will find it in you to exercise your faith and reach the utmost height of your capabilities. After all, "faith without works is dead." "The Lord has opened unto you His good treasure and has blessed the work of your hands. He has commanded the blessing upon you in your storehouse and all that you undertake."

Isn't it amazing that the God who made us also gave us the perfect manual that will allow us to live extraordinary lives? It is unfortunate that many will hear and not heed or take action. On our journey together I will be sharing much wisdom from the book of Proverbs, as well as other books in the bible, both the New International Version (NIV) and the King James Version (KJV). I will also share some real examples and stories in this book. The names of the characters have been changed, but the situations are real.

1

THE INSPIRATION

A few years ago, I joined a group of 21 other individuals to launch a new church. Over a period of about six years, the group grew to 84 faithful members. As we were slowly but surely outgrowing the space we had rented, we decided it was time for us to launch a campaign to raise some funds to have a space of our own. We needed more space and extra time than the current facility could accommodate, in order for us to enhance our community outreach ministries. We held a few fundraising events, concerts, bake sale, and bottle drives. Our efforts soon enable us to realize the goals we had set of raising $100,000. Though this was a good start, it was a far cry from the three million dollars ($3M) needed to fulfill our dream. It soon became very apparent that in order to realize our goal, we had to find more strategic ways of enriching our funds in order to maximize our efforts and get a better yield. It was then that my passion for teaching others how money works by following biblical principles was born. My zeal for helping to create funds to build a church was instrumental in getting me started as a Financial Educator with a passion to help families build a lasting legacy of change for future generations.

I thought that by showing acquaintances how to build wealth and how to reach their financial goals, they would experience an increase in their income. And as they exercised their faith and applied the principles, an experience of abundance would be generated among the membership, which would then produce an increase sufficient to fund the church building project from their giving.

The task of getting people to be interested in learning these principles presented a greater challenge than I anticipated. First, I began to lead by example in building a strong financial foundation for my family. I thought, if I could help at least ten (10) other families in the church to increase their income by an extra ten thousand dollars ($10,000) every month, then we would reach our goals much faster. As a church leader, I knew a lot of people who trusted me to pray for their varying situations, and to help them in many other ways, but none were willing to trust any financial advisor outside of the bank with their finances. I knew that the information I had to offer was valuable and well needed, but I had to find a way to share it while building trust. So I decided to consult the Master, who gave me the inspiration of using His word to open the eyes of His people. He has led me through many paths, some of which I had journeyed many years ago, before I even thought of writing it all in a book. This goes to show that our Creator knows everything and that He has a plan and a path all mapped out for each of us. The path of blessing has been prepared, it is waiting for you to be ready to receive it.

I will quote from the book of Proverbs as well as other books that will highlight the areas pertinent to our financial health. Though some may say that God does not need money, the management of money is very important to God. In the case of the Rich Young Ruler, Jesus told him to sell everything he had and give the proceeds to the poor, then come and follow Him. Does that mean everyone should sell everything they have to follow God? I would say yes, but only if it is a hindrance to your relationship with him.

This book is partially another effort to raise additional funds to support our church building project. I believe in offering value, whether I give it for free or at a cost. It is my direct intention that this book will change your life, dear reader, by helping you to think outside of the box, and as you develop your faith, enrich your life and that of the individuals in the communities in which you live wherever you are in the world. I will share with you 10 biblical principles that can help you along life's journey to have an extraordinary life of abundance while fulfilling your dreams and goals.

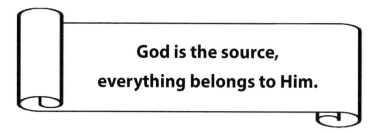

PRINCIPLE #1

Everything Belongs to God, He is the Source

I believe that one of the major themes of the Bible is obedience to the Lord. What is obedience? Generally speaking, obedience is when you do the things that you are instructed to do. When we speak to our children, we expect them to do as they are told. Biblically speaking: obedience is the fruit of righteousness. "For as by one man's disobedience many were made sinners, so by the obedience of One, shall many be made righteous." (Romans 5:19)

True obedience is an essential component in creating a close relationship with God. If you chose to be deficient in obeying God, you will lead a life of defect. We tend to look at obedience to God as following the Ten Commandments, but not very often do we even think that following God's principles about money would be at all very important. Obedience to God should apply to all areas of our life—the physical, emotional, spiritual, and the financial. The financial principles found in the bible are real, and obedience to them demonstrates that you do trust God in all other areas of your life as well.

Daily, I see people in deep financial trouble. Thousands in this country have gotten themselves into financial messes that can lead to more serious consequences. It is said that one of the greatest discoveries of this century is that you can change your life by changing the way you think. This wisdom, however, originally came from the bible. The way we think about monetary gains, and all other attributes of success for that matter, will determine which direction we take. The books you read and the people you associate with will definitely help to shape your future. It is said that over your lifetime your income will be ten percent (10%) of the total income of your ten closest friends. So it is good to surround yourself with people who can lift you and help you get to where you want to go, or help you stay on track to achieving your goals.

Seeking wisdom from God's word will surely enlighten and refresh your soul, and in this case, your pocketbook. "A good man brings good things out of the good stored up in his heart, and an evil man brings evil things out of the evil stored up in his heart. For the mouth speaks what the heart is full of." (Luke 6:45)

In Psalm 24:1, it says, "The earth is the Lord's, and everything in it; the world, and all the people in it belongs to Him". God is the creator of the world and everything that is in it. He has placed us as managers on the earth, and He has afforded us talents. We have different gifts, according to the grace given to each of us. "Each of us should use whatever gift we have received to serve others, as faithful stewards of God's grace in its various forms" (1 Peter 4:10).

"For I know the plans I have for you,"
declares the Lord, "plans to prosper
you and not to harm you, plans to give
you hope and a future."
(Jeremiah 29:11)

We are also promised a good supply of all that we will ever need. "My God shall supply all your needs according to his riches in glory by Christ Jesus." (Philippians 4:19)." (Proverbs 8:20-21) adds, "I lead in the way of righteousness, in the midst of the paths of judgment: that I may cause those that love me to inherit substance; and I will fill their treasures." In (2 Corinthians 9:8), it says: "And God is able to bless you abundantly, so that in all things at all times, having all that you need, you will abound in every good work." The silver is mine, and the gold is mine declares the Lord (Haggai 2:8) whenever we need money, possessions or direction; we should seek to commune with God through prayer. Look to the Lord because He will provide for you according to His will, according to his riches in glory. Your heavenly father is crazy about you whether you believe it or not. In God's eyes you are priceless; he loves you unconditionally and he also knows what is best for you.

"'For I know the plans I have for you,' declares the Lord, 'plans to prosper you and not to harm you, plans to give you hope and a future." (Jeremiah 29:11) God's plan for each of our lives is sure and well designed. In (Proverbs 3:5-6), it says, "You should trust in the Lord with all your hearts, lean not on your own understanding, in all your ways acknowledge him, and he will direct your path."

Our God is a good God all the time and He always honors His word. He never lies, and only desires for His children to walk in victory, wholeness, health, and abundance. (James 1:17) says: "Every good gift and every perfect gift is from above, and cometh down from the Father of lights, with whom is no variableness, neither shadow of turning."

God never turns from doing good for his children, and this is something we have to keep in the forefront of our thinking. He desires that each of His children have the good gifts that He chooses to give to us. He wants us to trust Him in all areas of our lives, and that certainly means our finances as well. He knows our needs; sometimes, He even answers before we ask. It is said that Solomon was the wisest man that ever lived, yet he trusted God to lead him. He was given wealth and prosperity even though what he asked God for was just wisdom and understanding. Solomon was totally committed to serving God in all aspects of his life. God has the unique ability to do everything He says. He is forever faithful, forever true, and forever sure. His word is true, and as (Proverbs 30:5) puts it, "Every word of God is flawless; he is a shield to those who take refuge in him." Are you ready to claim his promise for you?

> **God wants us to trust him in all areas of our lives, and that certainly includes our finances!**

What is your willingness to make a commitment to God? Are you willing to pray like it depends on God, and work like it depends on you? Pray while you are working. God has called you to cultivate the seed of faith in the area of work that he has placed you to enhance His will. We will have to do some work, as faith without works is dead. What good is it, my brothers and sisters, if someone claims to have faith but has no deeds? Can such faith save them?

Suppose a brother or a sister is without clothes and daily food. If one of you says to them, 'Go in peace; keep warm and well fed,' but does nothing about their physical needs, what good is it? In the same way, faith by itself, if it is not accompanied by action, is dead (James 2: 14-17). Deeply woven in our faith should be the idea of personal responsibility and the diligence to prosper. We must endeavor to eliminate fear, which is false evidence appearing real. "I sought the Lord, and he answered me and delivered me from all my fears." (Proverbs 34: 4)

In order to execute fervent action, we must first remember that all gifts come from God—we are mere managers, not owners, in spite of what we may think. "The land is mine and you are but aliens and my tenants." (Leviticus 25:23)

As a manager and steward, you also have to give a report of what you do to the one in charge. When you work for God and not for man, this will help you to do the right thing, give your maximum without expectation. So then, each of us will give an account of ourselves to God (Romans 14:12). Therefore, you should act what you say you believe, like you truly believe it, knowing that God is your source. Your behavior should be as if God is in the next room and can walk in on you anytime: after all, He is seeing all that you do. Commit to God today and invite Him to take full control, knowing well that He gives divine directives. Turn all your work over to God in prayer, and work with urgency to complete the task he has given you.

It is said that knowledge leads to prosperity, but it is the actual application of knowledge that will lead you to prosperity. Seek knowledge and wisdom from God through his word with supplication in prayer and acknowledge Him as your source, then work with diligence to accomplish the work.

Action Step #1: Pray the prayer that is appropriate for your needs and your situation.

Prayer: Father, I trust you with all my being. I know you love me even more than I can imagine. I commit my worship, my health, and my finances to you. I release my inner feelings of fear to you. Grant me the courage to do the things that are in obedience with your will, and help me to be faithful in all things. Amen!

2

PRINCIPLE #2

Get Out of Debt and Keep Out of Debt

One of the biggest myths of today is that you need credit to build credit. Who made that rule? You may find that it is the very same people who are providing you with the credit cards. The truth is, many individuals have become very sloppy in dealing with many things in their lives by leaving it up to chance. We get so comfortable in doing what everybody else is doing that we become lacking without even thinking about it. We need to realize that in the world as it is today, normal = stress. This is by no means what God wants for us.

"Do not be anxious about anything, but in every situation, by prayer and petition, with thanksgiving, present your requests to God, and the peace of God which transcends all understanding, will guard your hearts and minds in Christ Jesus." (Philippians 4:6-7). Imagine not having to worry about anything. The daily activities of life will cause you to worry, but we are encouraged to worry less and pray more. True peace will come from knowing that God is in control of our situation.

The Small Word with a Big Effect

Oftentimes, we get into debt because we are afraid to use one simple word that has worked over the years to solve so many problems. In fact, developing the skill of using this word, could be the most important personal, leadership, and professional development tool you will have in your toolbox. This is a word many of us despise because we are unwilling to accept what the reality of adhering to what such one small word can do for us and the change it can bring about, if we only stick to it.

That word is "NO."

Say *no* to getting the credit card, especially if you'll have a problem repaying when you use it. Unfortunately, we have that minimum payment mentality that will lead us into big trouble, so just say no.

Say *no* to the teenager who wants only name brand clothing.

Say *no* to the young adult wanting to get a Ferrari instead of an old Toyota.

Say *no* to using credit card to pay for something you want or think you should have only because your neighbor has one and you want to outdo them. As a matter of fact, I think right now is a good time to start thinking about becoming a plastic surgeon, by putting scissors to your credit cards.

Say *no* to getting the car loan that you will spend the next 84 months paying over $400 a month for, when you have no emergency fund.

Start Acting Your Wage

North America has created a normalcy in life that is called "living above your means." There is a constant need for greed. The need to get the latest gadgets and spend all your hard earned money to try and outdo each other. The right thing to do is to act your wage and stop spending money you don't have. Do you know what would happen to your situation if you saved that $400 over 84 months instead of paying for a newer car? That is $33,000 that could have been invested over time. If you invest that $400 per month from age 30 to age 70, you could end up with a whopping $5M. Wouldn't that make a very nice retirement you can look forward to?

I heard a friend tell a story of his wake-up call. He was driving his kid home from soccer practice when his son said he was hungry. As he got to the next fast food restaurant, and pulled up to the drive thru window, he ordered a burger that was for $1.37. He couldn't find any cash and had to pull out a credit card to pay the bill. He was overcome by and uneasy feeling of guilt, then it dawned on him how ridiculous his situation was. Here he was driving an SUV for which he was paying $700 per month in car loan, and yet, he couldn't afford a burger for $1.37. Many of us are no different; we get into debt to have the latest version of every gadget there is and impress people we really don't care much about anyway. What do you think would happen if we definitely act our wage, and live on less than what we make? We should adhere to the second principle, which is to **keep out of debt** and thus avoid the debt trap. What would it feel like if you have no payments, or what more could you do if you had no payments?

As Proverbs 22:7 says, "The rich rules over the poor, and the borrower is slave to the lender." Borrowing for a house is one thing, but taking on financial obligations you cannot afford by buying beyond the ability to pay is another. In an ideal world, the best way to buy a house would be to buy it with cash. But since we live in the imperfect world, the best thing to do is to plan ahead. Since circumstances that may require you to take on a mortgage, but you should plan to pay off that debt in the fastest possible time, using your amortization schedule. I would also encourage you to save a twenty percent down payment, which would drastically reduce the fees you pay. You would be able to save money on the insurance premium that you normally have to pay if you borrow with less than twenty percent down. Having that twenty percent down payment will potentially open many more doors for you as well. You could have the privilege of at least three options of funding your home. *(Please see your financial advisor for more details)*.

Did you know that a mortgage was actually designed for you to pay it off in five years? If you start out with twenty percent down, do a bi-weekly schedule, and pay down the annual allotted amount pre-payment, which can be 15 to 20 percent of the initial mortgage that you can add to your principal, you'd be quite surprised to see how soon you could get rid of that mortgage. Even with your five percent down you can pay your mortgage off in five years. The table below is an example of what would happen in two different scenarios, having the same mortgage with the same interest rate but with different amortization periods. You will see a huge difference in the amount of interest paid in each case.

Example of Accelerated Mortgage Payments

Mortgage = $300,000 @ 2.65%	Mortgage = $300,000 @ 2.65%
Amortization: 25yrs	Amortization: 5yrs
Bi-weekly payments: $629	Bi-weekly payments: $2457
Amount of Int. paid: $109, 681	Amount of Int. paid: $20,340
Total paid: $409,9681	Total paid: $320,0340
Balance after 5yrs: $254,809	Amount after 5yrs: $0.00

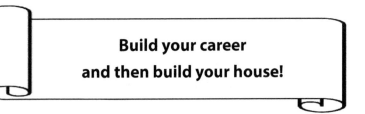

**Build your career
and then build your house!**

Build Your Career First

Many times we ponder the idea of buying a home as soon as possible. Yes, we need a place to live, however, the principles of the bible tells us to "put your outdoor work in order and get your fields ready; after that, build your house." (Proverbs 24:27) This is the best counsel ever—build your career first, and then build your house. This makes total sense as houses cost much more than they seem. When buying a house you need to consider the following: Down payment, closing costs, property taxes, insurance, heating costs and any repairs and maintenance that may need to be done to the property, as well as other utilities costs. Consider these things carefully and make sure you have a good reserve as an emergency fund for any unexpected expenses. Being unprepared for unforeseen circumstances may lead you into debt. You want to avoid the trap of being house poor. Buying a home is a major investment, but there is nothing wrong with waiting until you are ready to buy.

Avoid the Debt Trap

In (Psalm 37:21), it says, "The wicked borrows, and pays not again." The minute a person goes into debt, he loses a portion of his freedom.

For example: A couple with a $12,000 annual income had decided that instead of saving $1000 a year, they would go into debt for $1000 to buy some furniture or whatever else they think they must have. What if they chose to continue to increase their indebtedness by $1000 during each of the next 15 years, without paying back one cent? With ten percent (10%) interest, compounded annually, on the increase in debt, the couple's debt would have been an astronomical $34,949.74. The debt on $1000 alone for that same period, without any repayment, would have been just over $4000. We definitely know that ten percent (10%) is rather low, compared to the 19.9 percent and above that is charged on credit cards, and not to mention, the department store cards that are, in some cases, over twenty-six percent (26 %). For far too long, too many people thought they can buy now and pay later. We need to get rid of this mentality. The plan of the enemy is to keep us in a poverty mentality, having the fear of poverty and yet not doing anything to alleviate it. The truth is, what we think is relief in the short term will definitely come back to bite us in the long term and certainly dig deeper holes in our pockets.

Buy depreciating items only with cash.

What would you think if you saw someone driving down the highway, then rolled down their window, stuck a hand out full of $100 dollar bills, and opened their hand and let go? Crazy, right? Would you actually do that? I didn't think so! Well, that is exactly what you are doing when you use your credit card and carry a balance, paying the minimum payments just to be able to buy now and pay later. What happened to the idea of saving and buying what you need with cash when you need it? Where I grew up, nobody had credit cards or even a mortgage. Back then, you worked, saved your money, bought what you need, and build your house on land that you bought for cash. We should certainly go back to some of those habits of the good old days and the debt-free concept.

Think Cash First

When buying depreciating items, think cash first. You should strive to use cash only for these items. It is enough that you will be losing money from the depreciation. Why choose also to lose more by paying with credit? I've seen many instances where easy credit now makes the individual uneasy later. Usually, a person pays more for the use of borrowed money than they get in interest in a savings account, and that certainly puts them on the losing end of things. If you cannot afford it, do without it until you have saved enough to get it with cash. In other words, you need to control your debt, or debt will control you. Don't get more debt; live below your means. You can't spend more than you earn and expect to get ahead. That is total insanity. Use cash, or pre-paid credit cards if you have to use one. Being in debt can be an overwhelming feeling that you certainly could do without. In order to get out of debt, the first thing you need to do is make the decision to get out of debt and create a plan. Have a written plan to get out and stay out of debt and stick to it. Don't buy things you don't need with money you don't have to impress people you don't like. Is the feeling worth it? And even if that is not your motivation, you still need to be careful with how you spend your money by sticking to your financial plan consistently.

> **Looking at the way you handle money today, would you hire you to manage your company's money?**

Is the need to impress worth it? If you were the corporate money manager for You Inc. and you managed the company's money the way you handle your own money, would you still hire you? Would the company still be in business today? Individuals and companies alike will end up in debt for many reasons, and one of those reasons is fear, the fear of failure. We spend uncontrollably, sometimes to keep ourselves and others from failing. The examples we see around us are astounding. We hear of corporate bailouts and economy stimulation, all because we refuse to let the buck stop where it drops. We should love people enough to allow them to fail. Failure is one of life's greatest teachers. Failure is good in that it is, corrective, and instructive; it is cleansing, and will bring clarity to you and help define your purpose. If failure is chasing you, you will run toward excellence. Failure encourages and engages you to be your best.

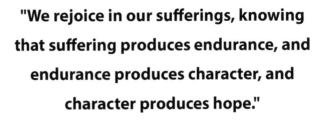

"We rejoice in our sufferings, knowing
that suffering produces endurance, and
endurance produces character, and
character produces hope."

(Romans 5:3-4)

"Therefore, since we have been justified by faith, we have peace with God through our Lord Jesus Christ. Through him we have also obtained access by faith unto this grace in which we stand, and we rejoice in hope of the glory of God. More than that, we rejoice in our sufferings, knowing that suffering produces endurance, and endurance produces character, and character produces hope, and hope does not put us to shame, because God's love has been poured into our hearts through the Holy Spirit who has been given to us as a comforter." (Romans 5:1-5)

So face your fears and use them as rocket fuel to propel yourself to greatness. Surround yourself with others who are of a like mind as yourself, and give gratitude always in all things, doing so with an attitude of compassion rather than an attitude of struggle. Spend more time cultivating your spiritual maturity, and realize that you are bought with a price and you are not alone!

Your Road to Recovery

In order to get rid of your debt, you have to start with a plan. You need to pay attention to what your debts are. You must first write them down, on paper and on purpose, and start listing them from the largest to the smallest.

- Make a list of all your debts and start paying them off one at a time, starting with the smallest to the largest. *(You could also start with the one that have the highest interest and get rid of it first.)*

- Start with the one with the lowest balance debt and eliminate it first, while making minimum payments on the rest, then continue trimming them one by one by applying all the money you used to pay the one before until they are all gone. *(You can then use that money to increase what you save and give.)*

Imagine yourself with no payments. The best place to be is in the debt-free zone. Did you know that one of the biggest money makers of the bank is interest charged on overdraft? That is daily compound interest. But you have been sold on the idea of security. In other words, it is ok to spend more than you make and live above your means—after all, you live to work for the bank, right? Living above your means will put you into overdraft, and this is one of the hardest habit to break. You are in debt because you are not using God's proven system of finance. The borrower is slave to the lender. Would you choose to live your life walking around with chains tied to your ankles? That is exactly what you are doing when you choose to be in debt. You are choosing to be a slave.

Slaves have no options; they have to do what someone else tells them. *I owe, I owe, now off to work I go.* You have to keep a job you hate, in order to pay the bills. You are totally maxed out each month, so you have nothing to give. As I have mentioned before, getting out of debt starts with a decision: you have to be responsible, have a plan, on paper and on purpose. Give each dollar a name before the month begins, and if you are married, you should do this with your spouse.

"The plans of the diligent lead surely to abundance, but everyone who is hasty comes only to poverty." (Proverbs 21:5) If you set your aim and ambition within the gifts that God has bestowed on you, and work diligently to achieve those goals, success is within your grasp. Diligence does not come easy to most individuals—it is a result of strong character, hard work, and persistence, and a strong character comes from being a humble and ardent servant of God.

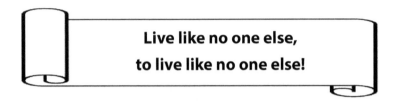

**Live like no one else,
to live like no one else!**

Have a Plan

"Write down the revelation and make it plain on tablets so that a herald may run with it." (Habakkuk 2:2) "Suppose one of you wants to build a tower? Won't you first sit down and estimate the cost to see if you have enough money to complete it? For if you lay the foundation and are not able to finish it, everyone who sees it will ridicule you, saying, 'this person began to build and wasn't able to finish.'" (Luke 14: 28-30)

If you have not acquired more than the bare necessities in your years of existence on this earth, and always have nothing to give, then you have failed to follow the principles that govern the building of wealth or you have failed to observe them. Remember the widow? Though she was considered the poorest in the society, she still gave of what she had. Being wealthy, however, does not necessarily mean you have millions of dollars in the bank. It means that you are able to live life to its fullest, and have the resources required when God calls you to a task.

There will be some that will laugh at your plan, and some will think you are crazy. Broke people will laugh at your financial plan, just as the overweight person will laugh at your diet plan. If you make a plan and stick to it, you will certainly reap the rewards.

Live like no one else, so you can live like no one else. Plan to get out of debt and plan to build wealth, so you will have a meaningful gift. Plan to give and have prosperity. It is good to have enough money to take care of the will God has for your life—that, to me, is prosperity.

"There will always be poor in the land, therefore I command you to be open handed towards your brothers, and towards the poor and needy in the land." (Deuteronomy 15:11) God implores us to respond to the needs of the poor. We ought to ensure that we are in a position to help when the need arises. It is said that one of the best way to help the poor is to not become one. When you are able reach out to those in need, you will be able to help your community to prosper and flourish while spreading the love of God to others. It is therefore good to stay out of debt, so you are able to help when the opportunity arises.

If at any point you have to borrow, be sure you examine your ability to repay it and pay the debt, or plan to pay it off as quickly as possible. Until your debt is fully paid, you are a slave to the lender.

I will also encourage you to also stay away from payday loans. This could get you caught up in an endless cycle of debt, as you are sometimes charged up to three hundred present (300%) in interest on those loans. Some statistics have shown even much greater charges. This will not only bring pain to you but also to your family. This is a trap, and a game that is not designed for you to win. I have seen it happen many times, and it is not a good place to be. Don't be enticed by the must-have-it-now mentality.

Action Step #2

Before you even start paying off your debts, build up a savings buffer of one thousand dollars ($1000). This is to take care of any unexpected expenses that may arise while you are paying off your debt. Though this may not seem like much, it can help you to avoid getting further into debt while paying off existing debts.

Ideally, you should continue to build a savings of up to 3-6 months of your income for a solid emergency fund.

3

Principle #3

Live on the Margins of Life

In today's world, we tend to overlook the need to create margins in our life. For our physical, spiritual, emotional, and financial well-being, we need to have margins. Having a margin is creating a space between your load and your limits. This means that you are making room for something to happen, by creating a buffer zone. Many times we tend to overextend ourselves, and this will cause us to feel overwhelmed.

Living on margin can be equated somewhat to temperance. You should be temperate in all things, not given to gluttony. You can create margins in different areas of your life: physical margin, a spiritual margin, a time margin, and a by no means least, a financial margin. Living on a margin simply means allowing room for things to happen so you are prepared when it does. "Be very careful, then, how you live, not as unwise but as wise." (Ephesians 5:15) In all things, seek godly wisdom and act on it.

Having a margin creates balance. You should refrain from becoming overloaded. Without margins in your life, you will end up being stressed.

Running on empty will get you nowhere. Having a schedule and sticking to it will help you create your time margins. Saying no to some things will help you create a margin for your commitments to help you avoid over-committing to responsibilities that could easily be delegated to others.

Jesus's life was a perfect example of a life on margin. Though thousands of people followed him and made various demands of him, he was never rushed. He knew how to prioritize and how to have a balanced life. Every so often, he would just slip away to have some quiet time with his Father.

It will take some effort on our part to create and maintain margins in our lives but this is an absolutely essential component of our well-being and prosperity, and it must be created. You have to be aware that sometimes, you will have to fight for your margins.

The Emergency Fund

In creating a financial margin you should first seek to build up an emergency fund. Having three to six (3-6) months' worth of your income in a savings account is ideal. You can chose to put it in a secure investment that you can access easily without penalty. Life will happen whether you are prepared or not. It feels much better when you are prepared.

Money is fun if you have some. As my grandmother would say "we should always save for a rainy day." You had better be ready when life challenges knock on your door; be prepared because they certainly will come knocking at some point in time.

You need to have a buffer zone between you and life. When things in life happen, many times I hear people say, "I don't have enough money to give," or "If only I had some money saved," or "I wish would not run out of money before the month is out!" or "I wish I could help." And many don't have any idea what to do or where to turn. Creating a financial margin in your life can help avert these feelings. In other words, you need some extra money each month just in case. If something happens, you need to know that you will be ready. You want to have the freedom to give, save and spend as God calls or instructs you to do so. Have the need to stop the stress you feel from not having margins, and give yourself some options.

What would it feel like to be able to go to a restaurant and give a large tip to someone in need of it? I recently went on a company reward trip to Mexico; I took my two daughters with me and they, being very observant, saw how diligently the people served us in every aspect of our time there. They served without complaining. Not knowing the culture of the people, we asked the young waiter, who served us so delightfully in the restaurant, if it would be acceptable for us to leave him a tip. He was so thankful and appreciative. Though a twenty-dollar tip on a free meal in an all-inclusive resort may not seem like much to you or me, it sure meant a lot to that server.

What would it be like if you could be prepared at all times to give, or to be able to pay the grocery bill for the next person in line at the store? One of the most freeing things we can experience financially is having options in the budget. Being ready and able to give no matter what life throws your way.

As I suggested to you in the action step of the previous chapter, before you start your journey to get out of debt, do what you have to do to save a thousand dollars in your savings account. This will create a buffer for you while you are getting out of debt. This is good to have just in case you need to call a plumber or need something else done in an emergency situation, you will be able to take care of it without going deeper into debt. That buffer will help you stay on track toward your debt-free journey.

The Good Samaritan

Another perfect example of being able and ready to act when you have a margin is told in the story of the **Good Samaritan** as recorded in (Luke 10: 25-37). On one occasion, an expert in the law stood up to test Jesus.

"Teacher," he asked, "what must I do to inherit eternal life?"

"What is written in the Law?" Jesus replied. "How do you read it?"

The man answered, "'Love the Lord your God with all your heart and with all your soul and with all your strength and with all your mind'; and, 'Love your neighbor as yourself.'"

"You have answered correctly," Jesus replied. "Do this and you will live."

But the man wanted to justify himself, so he asked Jesus, "And who is my neighbor?" In reply, Jesus said: "A man was going down from Jerusalem to Jericho when he was attacked by robbers. They stripped him of his clothes, beat him up, and went away, leaving him half-dead. A priest happened to be going down the same road, and when he saw the man, he passed by on the other side. So too, a Levite, when he came to the place and saw him; he passed by on the other side. But a Samaritan, as he traveled, came to where the man was, and when he saw him, he took pity on him. He went to him and bandaged his wounds, pouring on oil and wine. Then he put the man on his own donkey, brought him to an inn, and took care of him. The next day, he took out two denarii and gave them to the innkeeper. 'Look after him,' he said, 'and when I return, I will reimburse you for any extra expense you may have.' Which of these three do you think was a neighbor to the man who fell into the hands of robbers?" The expert in the law replied, "The one who had mercy on him. "Jesus told him, "Go and do likewise."

> **If I light a candle, and use it to light yours, my light will in no means diminish. By lighting each other's candle, soon the entire room will be lit.**

If the Good Samaritan had not created a margin, he would not be able to handle the opportunity God provided for him to minister to the sick. He paid in cash and promised to pay anything extra on his return. In this story, the stranger took the injured to the innkeeper and paid for his stay. If he did not give priority to honoring God's principles of financial success, would he be able to do that? The good news is that there are tremendous privileges when living debt-free so you can be in a position to help others. This option is available to us all. We just have to take intentional steps in managing our money well so we can get there. We need to have a vision for the future. Proverbs 29:18 tells us that, "Where there is no vision, the people perish." If I light a candle, and use it to light yours, my light will by no means diminish. By lighting each other's candle, soon the whole room will be lit. Many candles will make a luminous room. Let us therefore not look only for our own interests, but also for the interest of others.

Manage Your Income God's Way

God has entrusted you with much income over your lifetime, and he has also given you the choice to manage it in a way that pleases and honors him. You are not forced to allocate money to take care of debt and necessities with nothing left over. It is a matter of choice and obedience. The option to help others in need is available to you when you have a financial margin. Managing money His way is a test of true character and obedience to Him. Ask questions of yourself to see where your priorities lie. Is it with God or with material things? You should always remind yourself that money is only a tool to help you do God's work. Always use material things with integrity and put the interest of others before your own. Always deliver more in value than for which you receive in payment. This will separate you for the crowd and give you an exceptional edge. This is one of the most profound laws of nature.

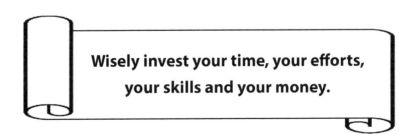

Wisely invest your time, your efforts, your skills and your money.

If It Sounds Too Good to be True, It Probably Is!

Many times I hear people say they have been scammed, and I wonder how that could have happened. Scammers have a pattern, and they are looking for people who are vulnerable to become their next prey. I spoke to a young man the other day who has been looking for an opportunity to go to another country to find employment, instead of looking in his own backyard. He recently graduated with an honorary diploma in his field, and instead of sending his résumé to companies that are looking for people with his skills, he went online and found a friend who promised to get him a job elsewhere. He made himself vulnerable and because of his desperation, he did not see the warning signs of the scammer, or he probably ignored the signs because he was so focused on finding the easy way out. He was scammed out of $30,000 dollars, which he had borrowed in hopes of paying it back after he got the job.

This scenario may resonate with some of you. It also goes against a few principles of godly wisdom. Proverbs 13: 13 tells us that "whoever despises the word brings destruction on himself, but he who reveres the commandment will be rewarded." In retrospect, we should avoid *Get Rich Quick* schemes. If it does sound too good to be true, then it probably is, so wisely invest your time, your efforts, your skills, and your money.

There are things and situations that are very real and come with extraordinary exceptions. Things like a debt forgiveness program that can, in some cases, wipe out up to 80 percent of your debt if you meet the requirements. That might sound too good to be true, but they actually exist. For this I recommend that you speak to your financial advisor regarding such programs that may be available to you, so you can learn of the options that might be available to you.

In the first book of Proverbs, Solomon, son of David, then king of Israel said, "Therefore to know wisdom and instruction, to understand words of insight, to receive instruction in wise dealing, in righteousness, justice, and equity; to give prudence to the simple, knowledge and discretion to the youth— Let the wise hear and increase in learning, and the one who understands obtain guidance." Be temperate therefore in all things, leaving a margin to respond to the unexpected things God may send your way.

Today I urge you to ask yourself this question: What margins should I set today?

Prayer: Father, teach me to be temperate in all things. Please guide me to make the right investment choices, so whatever I do I will honor you. Amen!

Action Step #3

In order to stay on track with
living on margin, set realistic
goals for both time and activity.

Write your goals and read them
them over daily. Be flexible
to adjusting your goals as
they will change. The goal you
achieve today will lead to a
different goal tomorrow.

4

PRINCIPLE #4

Save and Invest

I know a man who got really upset when he found out that his wife was saving a few dollars each month. He was so upset that he started withholding instead of giving her money to help with the expense of the home. She had tried over the years to work with him on a plan to save, but he was always saying he'd start saving when he gets a large sum of money. He didn't consider the small amounts he could have been saving each time he got paid. Truth is, he was a shopper. He shopped for gadgets, and while they were not the latest model, he would shop at PAWN shops all the time—he was a pawn shop junkie.

I think it was probably to fool himself that he was actually saving money since he was not paying full price, or so he thought. Most of the things he bought did not last long anyway; they were either defected or soon became useless after a short time. This man was just a shopaholic. He refused to save and was always waiting to receive more so he could save big, but that is totally not in line with God's principles. If you are not faithful in small things, for sure you will not be faithful in the bigger things. (Luke 16:10)

"Whoever can be trusted with very little can also be trusted with much, and whoever is dishonest with very little will also be dishonest with much."
(Luke 16:10)

When it comes to matters of money, our integrity is often tested and tried. God calls us to be honest in all our dealings. Whether it is with little or much, failing in the small things on earth is a sign that we are not ready to handle the larger decisions in matters that God may entrust us with. Keeping your integrity intact will enable you to have success in more crucial times later. Whoever can be trusted with very little can also be trusted with much, and whoever is dishonest with very little will also be dishonest with much.

We should always strive to do what is pleasing to the Master in all areas of our lives. "But whoever looks intently into the perfect law that gives freedom, and continues in it—not forgetting what they have heard, but doing it—they will be blessed in what they do." (James 1:25) While life is a gracious gift from God, we should seek to honor him through faithful obedience.

If you were born poor, it is not your fault, as there are things about you and your origin you cannot control. However, if you die poor, then it is totally due to your choices.

Over your lifetime, God will entrust you with a large sum of money. If you earn $60,000 per year and your working life is 40 years, you would have earned a total of $2.4M. Wouldn't it be sad if at the end of the 40 years you retired broke? This is the stark reality for many families and individuals today. It is said that if you were born poor, it is not your fault, as there are things about you and your origin you cannot change or control. However, if you die poor, then it is totally your fault, as you would have had opportunities that you did not take advantage of, or you did not live within your means and saved for the future. Even though we live in a country that is considered one of the wealthiest in the world, yet only one percent (1%) of the population retire wealthy, about five percent (5%) will retire comfortably, and the remaining ninety-four percent (94%) will retire below the poverty line. What is the difference between the six percent (6%) and the ninety-four percent (94%)?

They understand how money works and allow the money that God has entrusted them with to work for them as they follow God's proven plan of action in his principles of how to handle their finances. What if from that $2.4M you earned, you never returned a portion back to God? I have seen time and time again where God has miraculously provided for those who have been faithful to him while those who never return a faithful tithe always end up in want.

As I've said before, God's promise is sure; "I was young and now I am old, yet I have never seen the righteous forsaken nor their children begging bread." (Psalm 37:25) "Honor the Lord with your substance and the first fruit of your increase." (Proverbs 3:9)

I have been associated with many millionaire mentors, whether through their books, at a live seminar, or in person, and all of them have these three things in common:

1. They have the belief that God is the source of everything they have.

2. They create a written plan, work hard, and stick to it.

3. They give back to the community or to some charity.

This, my friend, is having the proper vertical and horizontal alignments that will lead to true prosperity in building wealth, faith, business, and family. And as they have been faithful in managing what they have been blessed with, their blessings increased. As Luke 16: 10-11 states, "One who is faithful in very little is also faithful in much, and one who is dishonest in very little is also dishonest in much. If then you have not been faithful in the unrighteous wealth, who will entrust to you the true riches?"

The Parable of the Bags of Gold

The story is told of a man who was going on a journey, so he called his servants and entrusted his wealth to them. To one he gave five bags of gold, to another two bags, and to another one bag, each according to his ability. Then he went on his journey.

The servant who received five bags of gold went out at once and put his money to work, gaining five bags more. The one with two bags of gold gained two more. But the servant who received one bag went off, dug a hole in the ground, and hid his master's money. After a long time, the master of those servants returned and settled accounts with them.

The man who had received five bags of gold brought the other five. "Master," he said, "you entrusted me with five bags of gold see, I have gained five more." His master replied, "Well done, good and faithful servant! You have been faithful with a few things; I will put you in charge of many things. Come and share your master's happiness!"

The man with two bags of gold also came. "Master," he said, "you entrusted me with two bags of gold; see, I have gained two more." His master replied, "Well done, good and faithful servant! You have been faithful with a few things; I will put you in charge of many things. Come and share your master's happiness!"

Then the man who had received one bag of gold came. "Master," he said, "I knew that you are a hard man, harvesting where you have not sown and gathering where you have not scattered seed. So I was afraid and went out and hid your gold in the ground. See, here is what belongs to you." His master replied, "You wicked, lazy servant! So you knew that I harvest where I have not sown and gather where I have not scattered seed? Well then, you should have put my money on deposit with the bankers so that when I returned, I would have received it back with interest."

This proves that God wants us not only to save for a rainy day but also to invest. God has given us gifts of time, skills, and many other resources according to our ability, and he expects us to invest wisely until he returns. Our responsibility is to use those gifts well. It is not about how much we have, but what we do with what we have. Wherever we are placed by God in this life or whatever we are given, we should diligently use all to His glory.

There is wisdom in storing choice oil.

Proverbs 21:20 says, "The wise store up choice food and olive oil, but fools gulp theirs down." And Proverbs 22:3 emphasizes that "The prudent see danger and take refuge from it, but the simple keep going and pay the penalty." Many individuals try to save money when they have massive debt, and find themselves in an endless cycle. It is wise to eliminate debt and then save to maximize gains. If you are saving money at five percent (5%) gain while servicing a debt with nineteen percent (19%) interest, say in this case a type of a credit card debt, you would be at a fourteen percent (14%) loss over the time of your debt repayment. It would certainly make more sense to get rid of your debt first, and then start saving and investing. Understanding how money works is the key to building financial wealth. People who don't understand how money works will end up working for money all their lives, while people who understand how money works will let their money work for them. We have to shake the myth that says if we become wealthy, we will be hindering someone else. The truth is, there is enough wealth out there for everyone to live a wealthy and prosperous life.

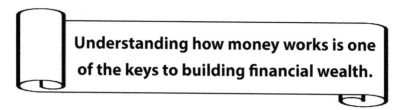

Understanding how money works is one of the keys to building financial wealth.

The Formula for Building Wealth

	Your Money	Amount of lump sum + regular deposits
+	The length of time	Period of time to allow your investment to grow
+/-	Percentage return	Rate of return (ROI)
-	Rate of inflation	Average inflation about 3%
-	Taxes paid on investment	Taxes owed on investment growth
=	Your wealth	Total investment in the end

Money takes time to grow. Money over time multiplied by the rate of return, minus inflation and taxes will equal your wealth. When you have a strong financial foundation, you are able to give more to others and create a bigger impact, as you exhibit godly wisdom in that which God has gifted you. If you have not started a savings plan, it is not too late to start. Better late than never. Not only should you save, but it is very important to start saving early, so now is a good time to start.

Start Saving Early

I always encourage young people to start saving early. Some of them will save to buy what they need for cash in the short term, but find it hard to actually save in an investment plan for the long term. A typical twenty-four year old who starts to save early will be in a much better position than his friend who may decide to see the world first, and then start saving six years later. Marla is a typical twenty-four year old who made the decision to start saving ten dollars per day ($10/day) instead of buying lunch. She decided to take the extra few minutes before going to bed at night, and pack herself a lunch for the next day. This provided three hundred dollars ($300) monthly investment in her future. She saved for six years and was able to find an investment vehicle that gave her eight percent (8%) rate of return. At the age of thirty, Marla realized a savings of $21,600 with a gain of $5,940, having a total of $27,540 in her investment. However, if she leaves that investment to grow for the next twenty years without adding any more to it, she will have $128,363 by age fifty. If she continues to add that $300 for the full twenty-six years, she would have contributed $93,600 over twenty-six years, and her investment would have grown to $298,243. She would be well ahead of her friend who, being the same age as Marla, started saving later at age thirty. By age fifty, he would have only accumulated a total of $170,798. Marla's investment would have grown by $204,643 while her friend's would have grown to only $98,700. Do you see how different the outcome is in the six years that it took Marla's friend to make the decision to start saving? Does it pay to wait? Certainly not! Spending is a habit, and saving is a habit. It is never too late to start a good habit, so start a good financial one now by saving today!

Example

Saver #1 - Started at age 24 Showing result at age 50	Saver #2 - Started at age 30 Showing result at age 50
$300/mth @ 8% return in 26 years	$300/mth @ 8% return in 20 years
Total Contribution	Total Contribution
=$93,600	=$72,000
Growth	Growth
=$204,643	=$98,700
Total=$298,243	Total=$170,700

Start building the good habit of saving now. If you save three hundred dollars ($300) per month, that is ten dollars ($10) per day for the next thirty years; assuming an 8 percent rate of return, you could retire with close to half a million dollars in savings. What if you are able to do only half of that, or even better, what if you are able to double that effort?

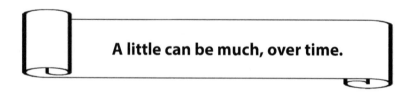

A little can be much, over time.

You are definitely richer than you think. It is high time you take full responsibility for your actions and for your future. Why should you work for forty years and expect the government to take care of you? Gone are the days of that kind of security, of false security, I should say. Forty years ago there used to be at least forty persons paying into a pension plan for one person to receive retirement benefits. Now there is only three and might be even less by the time all the baby boomers have retired, or even by the time you are reading this book. Do you think there will be money for you when you retire if you do not make the conscious decision to change something now? In the country I currently live in, there is only one thousand and sixty-five dollars ($1,065) available to you if you qualify for full retirement. How far will that go in this day and age? The purchasing power of the dollar will be reduced even further, twenty years from now. You need to know the secrets of building wealth and learn how money works, by adhering to God's principles of finance. Remember, saving and hoarding are not the same. A saver will also give, but the hoarder will save but never gives. You have to find that balance, which allows you to adhere to the principles of God.

Did you know that if you save $2.50 per day instead of buying a hot beverage daily, you are actually saving $75 over 30 days? That would be $27,000 over 30 years, and if that is invested at ten percent (10%) rate of interest, it would become $155,000. *(This of course does not take into consideration any fees for investing.)* But would that be a good deal? No matter how small the amount may seem, it can grow to something substantial over time.

One of the Best Kept Secrets of the Wealthy

James was an ordinary guy. He was only in his early fifties, and was retired with an income of over ten thousand dollars per month. I was very curious, and wanted to know how he did it. James worked as a sales person by day, and as a janitor at night. His wife Jeanette worked as an administrative assistant at a doctor's office. They have two children whom they love very, very much. James had a friend who talked to him about saving for his children's education. Though things were sometimes very tight, James thought it was a good idea. He then had his friend come to talk with Jeannette and himself about different options of saving for the children's education. His friend did a financial needs analysis for them and shared the option of having RESP, RRSP, and something called **universal life.**

A Bit about Universal Life (UL)

The universal life is an insurance product that has a saving and investment component attached to it. This product is offered only by life insurance companies and sold through their qualified advisors, and not by the bank. If structured properly, this could be one of the best vehicles to build wealth for retirement, as the income you could get from this is tax free. This product can also offer living benefit. This means that in certain circumstances, you can actually get some of the money available from this arrangement while you are still alive. As the concept was explained to James, he was willing to make the sacrifice to put some money away, for the children's college fund. He thought, at first, that he would have to sacrifice saving for their retirement in order to save for their children's education.

As James and his wife were being educated on the concepts of a universal life insurance product, and as it was explained in more detail, they realized that if structured properly, they could have the opportunity to realize both of these goals: saving for the children's education and having a retirement fund. They also learned that the children could get the money when they are ready to use it without being taxed. It amazed them to know they had the option of having the money when the children were ready to use some of it to pay for their education, and that it was tax free. The thought excited his wife Jeannette, and she offered to contribute an additional fifty dollars per month from her personal allowance to the fund. After all, the children were only one-and-a-half and three years old, and they chose the option to only contribute to the plan for twenty years. James fully understood the discipline it would take to make this a reality.

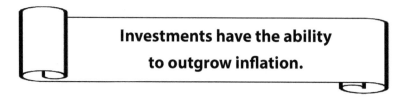

**Investments have the ability
to outgrow inflation.**

For a short period, James had a bit of struggle to meet the payments when he was laid off, but he worked with his advisor and together they worked out a way for him to make his minimum payments necessary to keep his plan in force.

James and his wife did their best to make the payment. Before you know it, the children were out of high school and ready for college. It so happened that the children were able to secure grants as they had high academic achievements. The accumulated cash fund was available to them, but they did not need to use it. Though no other contributions were made, James and Jeannette were able to retire and live comfortably on the interest, pulling in about ($10,000) ten thousand dollars per month from their gains, tax free from the accumulated growth of the funds. Though it was a sacrifice for them to stick to their plan at times, they chose to live like no other, so now they can truly live like no other. They were able to retire at a young age, due to the effect of compounding interest applied to their investments.

> **Which would you rather have,
> $100,000 today or a penny doubled
> every day over the next 30 days?**

The Concept of Compounding Interest

Do you realize the concept of compound interest? Ever heard the story of a penny a day doubled over 30 days? Though you start with just one penny, after a period of thirty days of doubling, the result is over five million dollars ($5M). That is the magic of compounding interest. Isn't it amazing? Sad thing is that ever so often, we chose to pay our debts as compounding interest instead of making our money work for us in compounding interest. Many lenders use this method when lending even your own money back to you. Yes, you heard me right—the banks take your money and give you between 0.25-2.00 percent, and then give you a credit card at 19.9 percent daily compound interest. As seen in the chart below, a penny a day doubled over thirty days will be over $5M, and by day 31, would be over $10,700,000. You see, with the magic of compounding interest, it is good to have your investments compounding interests but certainly not your debt. Watch what happens to this penny over 30 days! We are assuming it doubles every day, that is, $100% ROR (Rate of Return).

The Beauty of Compounding Interest on Savings

Day 1	$0.01	Day 16	$327.68
Day 2	$0.02	Day 17	$655.36
Day 3	$0.04	Day 18	$1,310.72
Day 4	$0.08	Day 19	$2,621.44
Day 5	$0.16	Day 20	$5,242.88
Day 6	$0.32	Day 21	$10,485.76
Day 7	$0.64	Day 22	$20,971.52
Day 8	$1.28	Day 23	$41,943.04
Day 9	$2.56	Day 24	$83,886.08
Day 10	$5.32	Day 25	$167,772.16
Day 11	$10.24	Day 26	$335,544.32
Day 12	$20.48	Day 27	$671,088.64
Day 13	$40.96	Day 28	$1,342,177.28
Day 14	$81.92	Day 29	$2,684,354.56
Day 15	$163.84	Day 30	$5,368,709.12

The rule of 72 was invented as a shortcut way to see how long it will take to double your money when you invest it. Seventy-two divided by the rate of return (ROI) is equal to the number of years it takes for your money to double. For example,

72/2= 36

Unfortunately, this rule works the same way with money you owe. From the example shown above, if you have a credit card at 19.9 percent interest with a balance of $3,000, you would pay twice the amount of that balance every 3.6 years; meanwhile, if you gave the bank $10,000 as an investment, and you get two percent (2%) interest as the return on your investment, it would take 36 years to double your money to $20,000. How many doubling periods do you have left? So why not learn how to get the same rate of return as the bank by shopping where they shop? It is good to earn compounded daily interest by making your money work for you, but certainly not good to repay your debt with compounding daily interest. When using compounding interest, your balance adds up faster than you think. Having a few dollars in savings with compound interest could mean the difference between poverty and financial comfort.

Using the Rule of 72

Here is another example that makes much sense to me:

Imagine a nineteen year old having ten thousand dollars to invest. Assuming a ten percent (10%) return on investment (ROI) by the time he is at the age of 68 years, he would have $1,480,000 if he left that investment untouched for the full 49 years. You may wonder, where would a nineteen year old get their first $10,000 to invest?

As a privilege of the wonderful country we live in, each Canadian child gets at least $60 per month from the Government for child tax benefit. This is paid to the parent with the lower income for the first eighteen years of the child's life, as long as the parent filed an income tax return. Over the eighteen years, the parent would receive $12,960. When the young adult reaches 18 years old, they become eligible to contribute to a Tax Free Savings Account (TFSA).

Example of Compounding Interest Using the Rule of 72
(please note, this is a hypothetical example)

Assuming a $10,000 investment at age 19 with approximately 10% ROR (Rate of Return), assuming investment doubles every 7 yrs.

- Age 19 = $10,000
- Age 26 = $20,000
- Age 33 = $40,000
- Age 40 = $80,000
- Age 47 = $160,000
- Age 54 = $320,000
- Age 61 = $740,000
- Age 68 = $1,480,000

About TFSA

This is a savings account in Canada that the Government allows each individual eighteen years of age and older, to save a total of $10,000 each year and the interest their money earns is tax free. The maximum contribution as of January 2015 is ten thousand dollars; however, if you have never contributed to this account, from its inception in 2009, and you were eighteen years or older at that time, you are eligible to put over $40,000 away and gain interest tax free. This annual limit has since been reduced to $5,500 as of January 2016. This is another wonderful account that you can use to access different vehicles to build wealth. The unused room for this account is carried forward to the next years so you can contribute the maximum. So of the $12,960 accumulated over the child's first eighteen years of life, you can have the initial start to your investment and it won't cost you a penny from your own pocket.

The key is, whenever you come into extra money, do not be quick to spend it. Try to find a way to make it work for you. When you receive a tax refund, remember, it is not free money. It is money that you have already earned that was sitting idle, so here is your chance to put it to work for you. Seek the knowledge to understand the multiplying effect of money. You will find that no matter how hard you work, your money can work harder and provide better yields to give you the lifestyle you deserve. Be money smart! Learn the basics!

What is TFSA?

TFSA means Tax Free Savings Account. However, TFSA is an account and not an investment. Talk to your financial advisor about different investment vehicles that you can use for your TFSA to get the best return. Another thing to consider is the advantage of vehicles where your investment will bypass probate in the event of your demise. It is very ironic that we are in one of the richest countries of the world and still end up with so many problems with our finances.

I was recently asked the question: As a Christian awaiting the return of Christ, do I really need to build wealth? The answer is partly in the Parable of the Talents (Matthew 25). If there was no need to build wealth or invest, there definitely wouldn't be a full meaning to this story. To the servants who invested their talents, the master said: "Well done, good and faithful servant. You have been faithful over a little; I will set you over much. Enter into the joy of your master."

The one who had received the one talent also came forward, saying, "Master, I knew you to be a hard man, reaping where you did not sow, and gathering where you scattered no seed, so I was afraid, and I went and hid your talent in the ground. Here you have what is yours." But his master answered him, "You wicked and slothful servant! You knew that I reap where I have not sown and gather where I scattered no seed? Then you ought to have invested my money with the bankers, and at my coming I should have received what was my own with interest." We could therefore conclude that there is some wisdom in investing to receive growth.

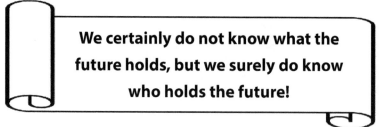

We certainly do not know what the future holds, but we surely do know who holds the future!

The Wisdom of Investing

Ecclesiastes 11:1-6

Ship your grain across the sea; after many days you may receive a return. (Ecclesiastes 11:1). Even the best-laid plans don't always work out—that's a reality we all have to face every day. So how should you live when you're not sure how things are going to turn out?

Solomon said, *"Don't play it safe—take some risks."* In other words, you have to live confidently. You can't hide just because life won't cooperate. Would you choose to avoid blessings because of the concerns that come with them? Would you say, "I can't get married?

What if difficult struggles come up between me and my spouse?" Or, "I can't have children. How will I know they won't be born with a birth defect?" Or, "I can't start a business. What if it fails?" Or, "I can't go to school. What if I never pass my exam?" We cannot control what happens, we certainly do not know what the future holds, but we surely do know who holds the future. God wants us to step out in faith and take some risks. He yearns for us to stop playing it safe and fully trust him. In life, sometimes the best of plans we have may fail. That, however, does not mean we should give up on life. What does it mean to cast your bread upon the waters? Firstly, notice Solomon in his wisdom in suggesting waters and not water. We could probably surmise that in the time of Solomon, he was very involved with international trade with other merchants. Trade was mostly done at sea, and most of the items traded were grains and other commodities. They would definitely not put all their merchandise in only one ship lest they lose it all at sea. If they lost one ship, then they would not lose everything. That is simply saying, diversify your investments; in other words, do not put your eggs in one basket. Ship your grain across the sea, and after many days you may receive a return.

Invest in seven ventures, yes, in eight; you do not know what disaster may come upon the land. (Ecclesiastes 11:2) There is no better time than the present to step out in faith. So stop procrastinating! Be diligent constantly. If you wait until you "have time" to do something you will never get it done. The "perfect opportunity" begins now—while you still have the ability. Don't put off what God has placed in your heart for another day. There is no perfect time to have kids. You will never have enough money, energy, or patience. Once you have children, don't wait for the right time to spend time with them. Before you know it, your kids will be all grown up. If you are married, don't wait for your husband or wife to be all that you want them to be. Begin pouring your life into your spouse now. Don't wait until you have spare time, more money, or better health. If you are a student, though learning never stops, seek to accomplish all of your educational dreams and goals today. Don't settle for mediocrity, just be at your best. Your success depends on you. If you are not currently ministering, get involved today. If you wait until you're less busy, until you feel right or ready, until just the right moment, you will never witness, never serve, and never see results. *Don't play it safe—step out in faith.*

If clouds are full of water, they pour rain on the earth. Whether a tree falls to the south or to the north, in the place where it falls, there it will lie. (Ecclesiastes 11:3) As humans none of us can predict or control the experiences or the events of our lives. You need to distinguish between those things about which you can do nothing, and those about which you can do something.

Since we cannot stop nature's patterns (when it rains or where a tree falls), we had better work on finding something else to do. The point is simple: Don't waste your time with God's affairs!

"The earth is the Lord's and the fullness thereof." (Psalm 24:1; KJV). Let God be God; He will concern Himself with His responsibilities. When we allow God to do his work, we will realize that all we have to concern ourselves with is doing our best in all that we do.

"Whoever watches the wind will not plant; whoever looks at the clouds will not reap". (Ecclesiastes 11:4) The farmer who waits for the most opportune moment to plant—when there is no wind to blow away the seed, when to reap, and when there is no rain to ruin a ripe harvest—will never do anything but sit around waiting for the right moment. And so, the seed will stay in the barn, and the ground will never be tilled. Solomon exhorts us not to be like the farmer that plants his seed, and though some fell on rocks and some fell on shallow ground, enough fell on good soil in order to reap a great harvest. Don't wait for conditions to be perfect, because that will never happen. It is true that the wind and rain might come and destroy the harvest, but there is a greater consequence for not planting the seed: you may starve to death. Today's work might be ruined and you might have to do it over again tomorrow, but that's okay. Today's work might succeed as well as tomorrows. And if so, then you will be able to reap the rewards for both. There is a song that echoes this very sentiment—you can spend your whole life building something from nothing, and one storm may come and blow it all away, but build it anyway!

As you do not know the path of the wind, or how the body is formed in a mother's womb, so you cannot understand the work of

God, the Maker of all things. (Ecclesiastes 11:5) Life is unpredictable and mysterious, so we have to take it as it comes. Solomon says life is just like the wind. God is the only one who controls the wind. Humankind cannot create or control it, for the wind is unseen and unknowable. We perceive its presence by its effects. Likewise, we cannot understand how God forms bones in the womb, but he is the Creator. His wonders are far beyond our comprehension, so we have to take this by faith; yet in doing so, we adhere to the most intelligent option available to us. It is clear that the creation of the human body could not have happened all by itself. God created man from the dust of the earth so, of course, since we cannot know God's activities, we have to take it in faith that He is the one who makes all things and knows all things and knows what is best for us. There are many times when we look at things that happen in the world and we don't have a clue as to what God is doing. But we have to trust Him because He is the one who creates and sustains all things. Too many times we freeze in our tracks because we don't know what God wants us to do.

We suffer from a paralysis of analysis; this is one of the most debilitating disease known to man. We over-analyze everything and think about the 'what ifs', and that only leads to inaction. We obsess over all the small things, the things we cannot change, and this leads us to be mentally deficient. We just need to trust God to lead and take action. Trust Him and take the leap of faith to move you to the next level. Any outcome from an action is better than the price you will pay for succumbing to the emotional weakness of fear and anxiety that leads to inaction. When you hear the nagging voice of uncertainty ringing in your ear or gnawing at your being, just learn to let go of your fears, let God take control and take action by doing your part!

Sometimes when you are faced with a decision in your life, you want God to tell you exactly what your choices should be. Does God have to tell you what to do? Will God tell you what to do? True communion with Him will lead you to make the right decision and the right choices. There is a difference between right or wrong decisions and right or left turns.

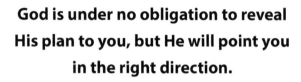

God is under no obligation to reveal His plan to you, but He will point you in the right direction.

In the Bible, the will of God always refers to moral choices—decisions where one path leads to sin and the other to righteousness. For these right or wrong decisions, right turns or left turns, you have to trust God to lead you to the path he has laid out in his plan for your life. You should seek his direction through prayer and reading of His word, and pursue the path of righteousness as he directs you to do so.

God is under no obligation to reveal His plan to us. More than likely, He will not reveal his plan to us, but he will point us in the right direction. That's why in the book of Ecclesiastes Solomon said you just have to be bold and act. We need to trust God more with our lives. Many times we pray for a sign, and sometimes even when we get the sign, we don't notice it.

There was a young man who prayed for God to touch him so he can know he is there. God came in the form of a beautiful butterfly and perched on his shoulder, but he quickly swooshed it away. Another prayed for rescue on a stormy sea. Three times God sent three different people to rescue him, he did not believe and sent them away, unfortunately to his demise.

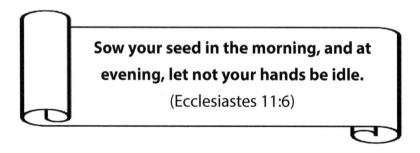

Sow your seed in the morning, and at evening, let not your hands be idle.
(Ecclesiastes 11:6)

It is imperative that you align yourself with God's plan and purpose for your life, and through faithful study of his word and prayer you will recognize the clues that will give you the information you need to show you which choices to make or which road to take. You just have to step out in faith, just simply trust him, pray about it, and then boldly follow your hearts' prompting.

"Sow your seed in the morning, and at evening let your hands not be idle, for you do not know which will succeed, whether this or that, or whether both will do equally well". (Ecclesiastes 11:6) Solomon issued a command: "Sow your seed," which is used metaphorically of giving, as in 2 Corinthians 9:6. Remember this: Whoever sows sparingly will also reap sparingly, and whoever sows generously will also reap generously. He wants us to have confidence and leave the results to God; that is what Solomon has encouraged us to do. What types of risks can you take or are you willing to take? Remember, there are endless possibilities, you just have to act.

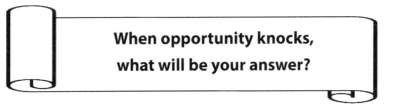

When opportunity knocks, what will be your answer?

Many of you have taken the leap from half a world away to come to North America. Would you say it is the Lord's leading that has brought you thus far? So why is it that you trusted God to bring you safely from halfway around the world, find you a job and a warm bed, yet you fail to trust him with your finances? It all belongs to him anyway, so why not trust him with it. Even you who are evil know how to give good gifts to your children, how much more so is the gift of the father who loves you unconditionally?

Some of the busiest people in the world have committed themselves to ministry even when there seem to be no time available in their schedule, but they trust God to make a way. He will open doors and provide opportunities for you to minister when you least expect it. As some individuals share their faith with others, they risk persecution, loneliness, and demotion. But through it all, God has guided and protected them as they do His will. They have learned to fully trust Him in all things. You can learn to trust him just as well, and allow him to use you for his glory.

After all, God is the master of all things, and he definitely knows what is best for you and how you should manage your affairs. The truth is, we are managers of what God has entrusted us with, while He is the owner of it all. And just like the foolish servant who did not invest the master's talents, what we have will be taken from us if we fail to manage it properly, or use it for his glory. Remember that God rewards faithfulness; there will be no reward if you do not bear any fruit. So use what you have well, so that it will not be taken from you. This will enable you to leave a true legacy of abundance as an inheritance. Are you shaping to leave a legacy of debt or one of abundance?

The Legacy Chart

What is your spiritual legacy?
What will you return to God?

Responsibility:
How will you provide for your families'
needs and your children's education?

Retirement:
How will you live when you retire?
What preparations are you making?

Have you built a solid foundation?

The Legacy Chart Explained

All things are from God, and therefore all things belong to Him. You have to give account of the gifts He has entrusted you with. As you live your life, there are a few things you should take into account.

Just like building a house, you need to build a solid financial foundation for your family. If something were to happen to you today, what would you leave your family? What about your mortgage, your debt, your children's education? Who will take care of your minor children?

1. What are your responsibilities to your family, and how will you take care of their needs? Will you leave them a legacy of debt or one of abundance?

2. What is your spiritual legacy, what will you return to God? How will you help to advance the projects that can help the cause of God? And what will you give back to your community?

3. How will you retire? Will you join the masses who are retiring in poverty or will you make the necessary preparations?

"A prudent man foresees the evil, and hides himself; but the simple pass on, and are punished."(Proverbs 27:12) These words caution us to safeguard ourselves against unforeseen circumstances. Seek to build a solid foundation for your family.

As you reflect on these things, you should seek to take the necessary steps to ensure these vital needs for your family are met. This can be achieved by honoring God every step of the way and in everything you do. Leaving a legacy is not about you, it is about your responsibility and commitment to those whom you will leave behind, those whom you hold dear. What would you like to be said about you? Think about it, what would you like to be written in the Lamb's book of life about you? "One generation shall commend your work to another, and shall declare your mighty acts." (Psalm 145:4) You should strive to leave this declaration of the wondrous and marvelous things that God has done in your life and through you as a legacy for future generations.

Action Step #4

Find a financial advisor who operates on Godly principles, and get a financial needs analysis (FNA) done to determine your financial need.

You will need a financial diagnosis before you can have a remedy.

5

THE BLESSINGS OF OBEDIENCE

As she walked around the boundary of her property, looking for a few branches of wood to start the fire, her thoughts wandered. She knew in her heart that this could be the last time she would have a real meal. She was down to a bare morsel. *I have just enough oil and flour to make a few cakes*, she thought, *this may be enough to last me and my son for a couple of days.* She was more worried about feeding her son than herself. She bent down to pick up a few dry branches. *This would be good enough to start a fire*, she thought. In her worship that morning, she had asked God to bless her efforts, and to bless her bowl and to help her to be strong and faithful in all things.

She was startled by a loud knock on the gate. She opened the door and was greeted by a stranger. "Hello," he said, "Please bring me some bread."

"As surely as the LORD your God lives," she replied, "I don't have any bread—only a handful of flour in a jar and a little olive oil in a jug. I am gathering a few sticks to build a fire and make a meal for myself and my son that we may eat it—and die."

Then the stranger said to her, "Do not fear; go, do as you have said, but make me a little bread from it first and bring it out to me, and afterward you may make one for yourself and for your son."

Though she was in want, her faith was tested to give this strange man of the little she had first; she obeyed, and because of her obedience, the need disappeared. She was promised that her jar would not be empty and her oil would not run out.

Sometimes, we are asked to give of what we have, or have the urge to give, but in our disobedience, we withhold and thus rob ourselves of the blessings in store for us.

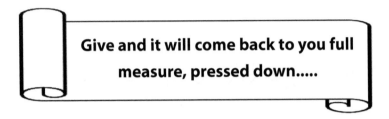

Give and it will come back to you full measure, pressed down.....

PRINCIPLE #5

The fifth principle is that of giving, giving is essential.

In Luke 6:38, a key verse, it says, "Give, and it will be given to you. A good measure, pressed down, shaken together and running over, will be poured into your lap. For with the measure you use, it will be measured to you." Deuteronomy 14:23 states, "Eat the tithe of your grain, new wine and olive oil, and the firstborn of your herds and flocks in the presence of the LORD YOUR GOD AT THE PLACE HE WILL CHOOSE AS A DWELLING FOR HIS NAME, SO THAT YOU MAY LEARN TO REVERE THE LORD YOUR GOD ALWAYS." According to this verse, one purpose of tithing was to teach the people of Israel to put God first in their lives, giving deep and sincere respect to him. What you do with your money will definitely show where your focus is, and what you value most. Taking some quiet time to pray and reflect is one way in which a person can honor God, and solidify their connection with Him through prayer and reading his word. I also believe another way to honor Him is by giving back. Proverbs 3:9 reads: "Honor the Lord with thy substance, and with the first fruits of all thine increase: so shall thy barns be filled with plenty, and thy presses shall burst with new wine." And 1 John 3:17 says, "But if anyone has the world's goods and sees his brother in need, yet closes his heart against him, how does God's love abide in him?"

Make Giving a Way of Life

For many years, I struggled with certain aspects of giving. Sometimes, it happened when I focused on the amount that I was supposed to give according to the word of God. Other times it was because of the mountain of bills I had to face, plus the pressure to make sure I had enough to feed my family. So I sometimes would not give the amount I intended because of my fear of not being able to pay the bills. It was not until I prayerfully asked God to guide my giving that I made a conscious decision to not only give the portion that God wanted me to give, but to go beyond and add more. I do this consistently now. No matter what I am faced with, I make it my duty to set apart my giving amount. It has become so embedded in me that it just happens naturally. It is then that I start to see things happen to prosper me time after time. In the past I had done it before, but then fell back into my old routine of inconsistent giving. Though I could see significant difference in the times I gave willingly and when I did not give, I still experienced the weakness of struggling to be consistent. Over time the habit developed and became ingrained, so that the consistency in giving becomes a way of life. I encourage you to try it.

According to Deuteronomy 14:23, one purpose of tithing was to teach the people of Israel to put God first in their lives. In God's word, the purpose of tithing is very clear. When we give God the first portion of our earnings, it demonstrates what we value most.

We sometimes hold back from giving because we do not know when, how, where, or why to give. Let us examine some ideas that may get you thinking:

When to Give – Consider your pay schedule for example, and also **establish a pattern of giving when your resources**

increase. This habit allows you to regularly remind yourself of God's faithfulness and to express gratitude to Him by giving regularly to meet the needs of others. A set schedule will develop a consistent habit, allowing you to develop strong Christ-like character.

Where to Give – Typically, the tithe should be given to the local church where you worship. These gifts support the pastor and the ministries of the church for meeting the needs in the community. As God prospers you and directs you, additional gifts can be given to other ministries that are advancing the Gospel. I have spoken to many givers who neither belong to any particular church denomination nor do they attend regular church services, but they find a church in their neighborhood or a local non-profit organization and give to them, to support a cause they truly believe in.

> **Give with the expectation that God will faithfully supply whatever you need so that you can abound in good works!**

What to Give – The tithe is **10% of your gross income**. In addition to giving 10% of your monetary income, consider giving God the first fruits of other resources as well, such as your time. It is very important to make it a habit of giving Him the first part of your day in a quiet time and taking one day in seven to focus on worship and rest. (In Genesis 2: 1-2), it says, "Thus the heavens and the earth were finished, and all the host of them, and on the seventh day God ended his work which he had made: and he rested on the seventh day from all his work which he had made." Invest your energies, gifts, and abilities in your church and community by giving back time as well as monetary gifts as the need arises. Tithing is one way to worship God—to honor Him as your provider and remind yourself that all of your resources belong to Him and are provided through His grace.

As you give to God the first ten percent of your income, you set your course to honor Him in the way you allot the rest of your finances. Tithing of ten percent is, however, the minimum testimony of our Christian commitment. You are in partnership with God. All throughout the bible, there are many examples of faithful people. Abraham was considered the Father of Faith. 'Thus all the tithe of the land, of the seed of the land or of the fruit of the tree, is the Lord's; it is holy to the Lord." (Leviticus 27:30)

As I have mentioned before, I have been coached by many multi-millionaires, whether through their books or in person, and there are three things they all have in common.

- They believe in God, although some refer to Him as a higher power.

- They have a plan and they put it in writing.

- They give back. Even though some may not belong to a specific church denomination, they find different ways to give.

How to Give – Your motives for giving are important to God. In (2 Corinthians 9:7-8), it says, "Each of you should give what you have decided in your heart to give, not reluctantly or under compulsion, for God loves a cheerful giver. And God is able to bless you abundantly, so that in all things at all times, having all that you need, you will abound in every good work." Give knowing that God will faithfully supply whatever you need so that you can abound in good works! He said it in his word, and His word is true.

Before I even thought of becoming a financial educator, I taught my children the 1/3 rule.

- 1/3 give

- 1/3 grow

- 1/3 spend

If your expenses are more than 1/3 of your income, you are heading for trouble; therefore, you should find a way to adjust them to be closer to the mark. The other rule of thumb is, you don't have to spend your full third, so you can use your unused portion of your spending to boost your saving or your giving or both. Unfortunately, this 1/3 rule does not stand once you have a debt to a service. That will totally change this ratio, and this is why we should be encouraged to stay out of debt.

Growing in the Fear of the Lord

The practice of tithing provides a regular reminder of your dependence on God. In good times, tithing helps you remember that God is the source of all blessings, and it allows you to demonstrate your gratitude for His care. In hard times, tithing motivates you to remember God's faithfulness, and it enables you to demonstrate trust in God to provide for all of your needs. In (Deuteronomy 14:22–23), God instructed the Israelites: "Be sure to set aside a tenth of all that your fields produce each year. Eat the tithe of your grain, new wine and olive oil, and the firstborn of your herds and flocks in the presence of the Lord your God at the place he will choose as a dwelling for His name, so that you may learn to revere the Lord your God always..."

Whatever your current situation, tithing is a key to learning to live in the fear of God. (Proverbs 11:24) states, "One gives freely, yet grows all the richer; another withholds what he should give, and only suffers want." In (Malachi 3:10), it says, "Bring the full tithe into the storehouse, that there may be food in my house. And thereby put me to the test, says the Lord of hosts, if I will not open the windows of heaven for you and pour down a blessing until there is no more need." When you develop the regular habit of tithing, it help you to keep God at the top of your priority list and enables you to have the proper perspective of all other things in your life. We can therefore conclude that giving is an essential component in the growth and maturity of your Christian walk.

Now is a good time to ask yourself this question: Who can I bless with a gift today?

Action Step #5

Prayer: Father help me to be a good steward of the finances, gifts and talents you have given me. Impress upon me the need to give willingly to help those truly in need. Direct me to those you need me to help today.

Amen

6

PRINCIPLE #6

Be Content with What You Have

What does it mean to be content? The dictionary meaning of the word content is to be in a state of peaceful happiness. The word content comes from the Greek word *artukes*, and it means to be self-sufficient, satisfied, or independent. In Philippians 4: 10-13, Paul expounds the word to show that he rejoiced in the Lord greatly when he received the gift, not because of the monetary gains but because it showed the Philippians' heartfelt love and concern towards him. Paul was not detached from people or from his feelings. He loved them dearly and was not afraid to show it. He established self-sufficiency as sufficiency in Christ, and not in worldly things. Unlike what some may think, contentment does not mean complacency. You can work to make a better life for yourself as different opportunities are presented to you. If you work hard, the reward will come as long as you are free from greed.

Therefore, be careful to be in constant communion with God in order to recognize his calling and that you are in submission to his will. If you are in an unpleasant situation, there is nothing wrong with seeking a better way out as long as it is in line with God's will and purpose for your life. Being content does not mean mediocre or not having the will to seek and exhibit your full potential.

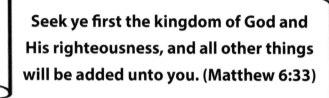

Seek ye first the kingdom of God and His righteousness, and all other things will be added unto you. (Matthew 6:33)

So as we adhere to the sixth principle of being content with what we have, (Hebrews 13:5) puts it succinctly: "Keep your lives free from the love of money and be content with what you have, because God has said, 'Never will I leave you; never will I forsake you.'" You have to come to realize God's sufficiency for your needs. In this day and age, everyone wants to get more of everything. We are constantly wanting to build up treasures on earth. As our inability to be satisfied continues, we live in a world where we keep purchasing more than we need. It is this hunger and greed that puts us into trouble most of the time. (1 Timothy 6:6-10) says, "But godliness with contentment is great gain. For we brought nothing into the world, and we can take nothing out of it. But if we have food and clothing, we will be content with that. Those who want to get rich fall into temptation and a trap and into many foolish and harmful desires that plunge people into ruin and destruction. For the love of money is a root of all kinds of evil". Some people, in their eagerness to acquire money, have wandered from the faith and pierced themselves with many griefs.

So give out of the abundance of your heart and relish what you have, rather than resent what you are missing. Money is a tool that will help us to complete the tasks that have been given to us. We have to keep things in perspective and not allow ourselves to be controlled by money and things.

The Secret of contentment

There is a secret to being content. No matter what situation you find yourself in, you ought to remain confident knowing that God has promised he will supply all your needs according to his riches in glory. "But seek first the kingdom of God and his righteousness, and all other things will be given to you" (Matthew 6:33). Fervent communing with God will allow Him to manifest His will in your life. In our own eyes, it is always better on the other side, but you will never know until you get there. Keep your eyes fixed on God instead of over the fence. A worthwhile saying to remember on contentment is this: "Use it up, wear it out, and make it do, or do without." Stop complaining, and instead, give gratitude in every situation. In Christ alone all hope is found.

Not that bad after all

There was once a man who thought his situation was worse than anyone else—he had lost his job, he had no family, and only had one finger of ripe banana left to eat at home. He climbed a tree and put a noose around his neck. "After all," he said, "I have nothing more to live for, and there will be nothing else for me to do as I have nothing to eat after this." He peeled the banana, and as he ate the last bit of it he let the skin fall to the ground. As he was about to jump, he looked down and saw a lone young man passing by, who stopped and picked up the banana peel.

After the young man picked up the peel, he knelt down and gave thanks to God for providing this meal. He then started to eat the banana peel as he walked away, rejoicing. The man in the tree realized his situation was not so bad after all, and changed his mind.

Sometimes, if we take our eyes off ourselves and our situation, we are better able to see the need to help others and also to show gratitude for what we have. Remember, God will not give you big things if you are not faithful in the small things. Instead of focusing on what we do not have, give thanks daily and be content in all situations. Do we really need everything the Jones's have? So be content in your situation, be content with what you have, seek to live daily in his presence and he will reward you richly. (1 Thessalonians 4:11) states: "And to aspire to live quietly, and to mind your own affairs, and to work with your hands, as we instructed you." (1 Timothy 6:6-8) says, "Now there is great gain in godliness with contentment, for we brought nothing into the world, and we cannot take anything out of the world. But if we have food and clothing, with these we will be content."

And as Paul, who was imprisoned, puts it in (Philippians 4:11-13), "Not that I speak in respect of want: for I have learned, in whatsoever state I am, therewith to be content. I know both how to be abased, and I know how to abound: everywhere and in all things I am instructed both to be full and to be hungry, both to abound and to suffer need. I can do all things through Christ who strengthens me."

So what does contentment mean? *It is an inner sense of rest or peace that comes from being right with God and knowing that He is in control of all that happens to us.* It means having your focus on the kingdom of God and serving Him, not on the love of money and material things. If God grants you material comforts, you should thankfully enjoy them, knowing well that it all comes from His loving hands. You should always seek to use it for His purpose and His glory, by being generous to those in need. If He takes your riches, your joy remains steady, because you are fixed on Him.

Contentment also means not being battered around by difficult circumstances or people, and not being wrongly seduced by those who appear to have prosperity. Let your life be centered in a living relationship with the Lord Jesus Christ. So no matter what happens to you or what others do to you, you should have the steady assurance that God will always be for you and He will not forsake you. Let us draw on the strength of our Creator to sustain us and take us through difficult situations.

Action Step #6

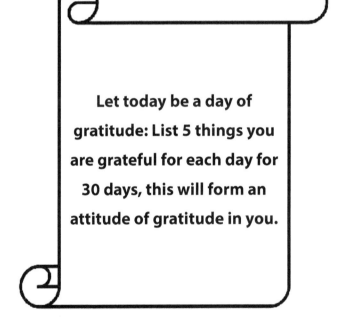

Let today be a day of gratitude: List 5 things you are grateful for each day for 30 days, this will form an attitude of gratitude in you.

7

PRINCIPLE #7

Keep Records, Make a Budget

The seventh principle is that of keeping records and making a budget. As God is the owner of everything, it would be fair to say that we are managers of the gifts that he has entrusted us. Paul said that it is required of stewards (managers) that one be found trustworthy (1 Cor. 4:2). I was taught that if I borrow or use something belonging to someone else, I should treat it more carefully than even my own things so that I can return it to the owner in good condition. That is especially true if the owner is God! It is very important for us to act as managers and not owners. We have to be faithful in all matters. If someone were to tell me that he's going to run his business without keeping any records, it would definitely not be very smart. And it is even worse for you who really wants to be a good steward of the Lord's money. How will you know when you are returning to God the correct portion if you never kept record?

As managers of God's assets, we should be responsible. Keeping of proper records will not only make you work more efficiently but will also enable you to be ready to meet any legal obligations if they do arise. You will be better able to make decisions more readily as you will have all the information you need at hand. God loves order, and we should seek to be orderly in all our doings as we are serving God and not man.

> **If we truly want to advance in terms of our responsibility in God's service, we have to prove ourselves Faithful in all matters!**

Be Faithful

In the book of Luke, chapter 16: 1-12, the point of being faithful in little money is highlighted in that God will give you more to manage if you are faithful in the small things. If you are faithful in the minutest jobs, God will give you a more important job to manage. In essence, money is referred to as the little things while much is referred to as true riches, namely the heavenly riches that cannot be taken away. The most valuable asset to God is the human soul. Our main purpose on earth is to help redeem mankind back to God and to worship and honor Him. The riches are the souls that have been won back to God. How can God entrust you with winning souls, if he cannot trust you with managing a measly earthly possession like money? Managing money is merely like a practice game, in order to prepare ourselves for the real wealth of harvesting souls for the kingdom. God will not put us in the big game, to entrust us with the spiritual overseeing of the souls that Jesus has purchased with his blood, the ultimate price, unless we prove ourselves worthy.

That is why the requirements for elders and spiritual leaders is to be good managers of their households, which includes finances. If you desire to be used by God in evangelism and disciplining of others, you have to be in obedience to God and get your financial life in order.

If we truly want to advance in terms of our responsibility in God's service, we have to prove ourselves faithful in the matters of money—and the Lord will give us true riches. In order to be faithful in our finances, we must therefore operate as managers of God's resources and not as owners. God's Word says, "Buy the truth, and sell it not; also wisdom, and instruction, and understanding." (Prov. 23:23) In (Proverbs 24: 3-4), it also says, "Through wisdom is a house built; and by understanding it is established: and by knowledge shall the chambers be filled with all precious and pleasant riches." Let us strive to be found faithful in all matters concerning our Heavenly Father.

Keep Good Records

If you owned a company and your managers never kept any records, I am sure you would agree that the business would be in utter chaos. By keeping good records, having a plan and being honest with yourself, you can avoid getting into financial trouble. I seldom see financially successful people who do not keep good records. No matter what system they choose, they do keep records. When you think of following Jesus, you probably don't think about keeping good financial records, but God wants you to keep track of what you spend, what you owe, and what you earn.

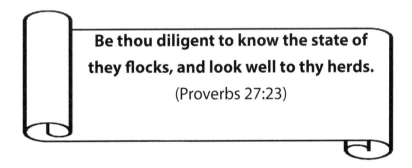

Be thou diligent to know the state of they flocks, and look well to thy herds.
(Proverbs 27:23)

The Bible says we need to watch our financial interests closely. "Know the state of your flocks." except today we might say, "Know the state of your stocks." In other words, you need to know where your money is going. People say money talks, but actually it just walks away quietly and you wonder where it went. Not knowing where your money is going equals disaster. You will get into trouble financially, especially if you're not keeping good records that show you exactly what is happening with your finances. You will be in constant turmoil as you wonder where it all went. Spending uncontrollably without knowing where your money is going can cause all kinds of problems in your life. When you start to wonder where it all went, that is a warning sign that you are already in trouble. In earnest, you need to put everything on paper in order to keep track. You need to know what you earn, owe, and spend. You have to keep good records, because riches can disappear fast. Think about this: If you spent as much time writing down your finances as you do worrying about them, you'd probably have a lot less to worry about. You need to keep good records if you want God's blessing on your finances.

There are companies that have lost thousands of dollars because they didn't keep proper records. Therefore, in all wisdom, keeping good records can keep you from having the headaches that will come from improperly recording and storing necessary information. It only makes good sense to keep proper records if you want to be faithful to God. It is imperative for you to keep a good record of all income and expenses, as proper documentation of invoices and receipts is very necessary and important for accuracy of how your taxes are calculated. It does not matter if you pay a specialist to help you with your affairs, you will still need to provide them with the necessary correct information. How else will you know if you are giving God his true portion? "And Jesus answering said unto them, "Render to Caesar the things that are Caesar's, and to God the things that are God's." And they marveled at him. (Mark 12:17)

Keeping proper records will allow you to be in true obedience with giving. God wants you to be wise with the assets he has entrusted to you. You should always plan ahead and use common sense so you are aware of the facts surrounding your enterprise including your finances. You will then be better able to manage these assets. Having a plan on paper for your assets is called a budget. The budget tells your money where you want it to go, rather than wondering where it all went.

I have created a simple budget sheet that you can use to start your journey. Make sure you allot the first twenty present (20%) to giving and saving. You can then adjust the remaining eighty percent (80%) to live by. You can make adjustments to the sheet to include any expense that is relevant to your situation.

The sample budget on the following page is to encourage you to put your plan in place and learn to live on less than you earn. If you have never made a budget, now is a good time to start. You can use a simple budget to get you on track for financial freedom. List all your expenses and your income. Put down the amounts you are actually spending each month for each item. Then have a column for what you should actually be spending on each item. You can start by putting a cap on the amount you want to spend for each item. Your income minus your expenses will give you your net. If your net amount is in the negative (-) you need to trim your expenses until you have some money left over. If you are still having a negative balance, you need to find different ways of increasing your cash flow. Even if you have a positive (+) net balance, you can still look for ways to trim your spending.

For example, eliminating a $7.50 dollars a day latte will give you an extra $225.00 per month to put into your savings. That $225.00 per month invested at eight percent (8%) over 10 years will yield you $40,789 dollars. Quite an expensive latte, I would say. I encourage you to take charge of your future. Only you can make the decision to do what is best for you and your family.

Simple Budget Worksheet

Monthly Expenses	Actual Amt.	Income	Percentage	New Amt.
Tithe			10%	
Savings			10%	
			80%	
Mortgage/Rent				
Utilities (light, heat, sewer)				
Child Care				
Food				
Auto Loan				
Credit Card				
Personal Loan				
Other				
Total				

Action Step #7

Starting today, make a budget, give each dollar a name on paper and on purpose. Make note of what you are actually spending and use the 20/80 rule to adjust your spending. Your eventual goal should be to increase the twenty percent (20%) giving and saving portions to a total of fifty percent (50%).

8

DO NOT CO-SIGN

A Lesson Well Learned

A friend of mine shared his story with me: He was asked to co-sign a loan for a friend. The friend skipped town when the payment became due. He was now left on the hook to pay a sixty-five thousand dollar debt. He was not able to pay all this debt at once and unfortunately the lender was so unforgiving that he had him taken to jail. Luckily for my friend, he had a very understanding boss who, on hearing of his employee's plight, loaned him the money to pay the debt so he could be released. He spent the next two years giving a part of his income to pay off that debt.

How much farther ahead he would have been financially had he not have to pay that debt? Refusing to strike hand in surety for another may not make you the most popular among your peer. However, if a friend encourages you to co-sign another's debt, it certainly would not be in your best interest.

In the book of Proverbs chapter 6, the warning is very clear against becoming accountable for another person's debt. "My son, if you have become surety for your neighbor, have given a pledge (hand) for a stranger," Solomon cautions us against being hurt by an imprudent friend or by a person we do not know well. Putting up security is referred to frequently in many other verses in

Proverbs. Even though God wants us to extend our hand to the poor and the needy, he does not want us to make unwise commitments that will cause our family to suffer.

> **The reason a person needs a cosigner for a loan is because he cannot afford the payments in the first place.**

To become surety for someone is to be a cosigner on a loan that is unsecured, and as a matter of fact, you are the security on what could be a high interest loan. Proverbs 22:26 warns against this: "Do not be one who shakes hand in pledge or put up security for debt."

The cosigner is responsible for the debt should the one who actually received the loan defaults or is unable to repay the loan in part or in full. When a person co-signs a note, he is the one who is really borrowing the money. The lender is unwilling to lend money to a person whom they see has a high risk of not repaying. The counsel of not co-signing is a caution directed against rashly stepping in to help or co-signing a loan for someone who is a high security risk. We should order our affairs with prudence and discretion, and many times that will force us to say 'no,' even when our emotions would like to say 'yes.' God does not want us needlessly in debt or responsible for someone who is borrowing with no means to repay. We should, therefore, carefully consider our actions and ensure they are in line with God's principles.

Principle #8

The eighth principle is **don't co-sign.** (Proverbs 27:13) calls us to exercise extreme caution in co-signing, as you could lose the very shirt from off your back. *Take the garment of one who puts up security for a stranger; hold it in pledge if it is done for an outsider.* The advice infers that the world's poorest credit risk is the man who agrees to pay a stranger's debt.

Don't be caught up in a snare. There are individuals who have entered into virtual promises without knowing neither how far they were pledging themselves nor all the elements concerning the financial commitment they have agreed to. It is easy to get yourself into these situations when you are caught up in the moment or in persuasive talk and do not seek the proper counsel. It is, however, not as easy to get out of, for it is a snare and now you have "been caught by your words" so you are now tied to that debt until it is paid up, and this could lead to serious consequences. The simple and naive are especially at risk, so be careful of any promises you make lest you cannot get out of it. Be honest and let the person know that you are living by God's principles and not your own. Saying no to them could be the best thing for them as well. If you have bound yourself with a financial trap of co-signing someone else's debt, you should frantically fight to free yourself of it. The basic premise is that it is the height of wisdom to keep yourself out of debt.

It is not beneficial in the long run for people in need to be helped into more debt. It is an entanglement and hard to get rid of, so this should be avoided. "The way of fools seems right to them, but the wise listen to advice." (Proverbs 12:15) If you know you should not go into debt for yourself, don't do it for another person either. It does not matter the pressure you are placed under to do so, it is not wise and definitely not worth it. Having the wisdom to refrain from co-signing is a favor to the other person as well as it is for you. Have the moral courage of doing the unpopular thing, as succumbing to pressure will be as detrimental for you as it is for them.

"You are bought with a price, do not become slaves of men" as stated in (1 Corinthians 7:23). God wants us to be free from debt and from sin. Many people say that slavery was a thing of the past, but truth is, being in debt is slavery. Why not chose to leave the past in the past? As we free ourselves from the slavery of debt, let us be cognizant of the fact that with the price paid on the cross, the powers sin and fear no longer have a hold on us as that debt also has been paid.

A Warning against Stupidity

The book of Proverbs provides many warnings to which we should heed. Proverbs 6:1-5 says, "My son, if you have put up security for your neighbor, if you have shaken hands in pledge for a stranger, you have been trapped by what you said, ensnared by the words of your mouth. So do this, my son, to free yourself, since you have fallen into your neighbor's hands: Go—to the point of exhaustion—and give your neighbor no rest! Allow no sleep to your eyes, no slumber to your eyelids. Free yourself, like a gazelle from the hand of the hunter, like a bird from the snare of the fowler."

My friend has learned his lesson the hard way. Take heed, therefore, and though you may be unpopular, it is better to be unpopular with man while following the principles of God than to be popular with man and be in disobedience with God. The prudent sees danger and hides himself, but the simple go and suffer for it. Many people are destroyed for lack of knowledge; let us not forget the laws of God, but faithfully adhere to them.

Action Step #8

Pray for God's wisdom when making decisions. Consider following the principles of God in all you that you do. Show biblical proof so others will realize it is God who is in charge and not you.

Learn to say No!

9

Work Hard/Work Smart

There are many individuals who work very hard and some who are just plain lazy. No matter what category you fall in, if you are working hard but never seem to get ahead, or if you think you are being true to yourself but is still falling short, you have to acknowledge the need to gain wisdom from God through the seeking of knowledge. As we examine the wisdom set out in the following reading from (Proverbs 6: 6-11), it becomes quite clear that we can all learn something from the Ants.

> *Go to the ant, you sluggard; consider its ways and be wise! It has no commander, no overseer or ruler, yet it stores its provisions in summer and gathers its food at harvest. How long will you lie there, you sluggard? When will you get up from your sleep? A little sleep, a little slumber, a little folding of the hands to rest—and poverty will come on you like a thief and scarcity like an armed man.*

These lessons in Proverbs are teaching us how to live like the ants. Even though they have no leaders, or supervisors breathing down their neck, they go about their way preparing for the winter. They store enough food from the harvest to take them through the long winter months. Have you ever watched an ant that has just found a crumb? He examines it, and if it is too big for him to carry, he goes back for help. Pretty soon there is a long line of ants coming to help. They work unitedly and all towards a common goal. They definitely work hard as well as work smart.

What Does the Ants Teach?

These are some things we can learn from the ants:

1. **To be hardworking**: Very often we see the ants lined up on a daily basis. They are always working hard, especially in the summertime. Have you ever gone to a picnic and left any food that may have fallen unattended? In an instant, there will be a whole colony of ants working together to get all that food in storage. They will not wait around but will work diligently to get the job done. Day and night, they work and it does not matter who sees them, or who may put any obstacles in their way, they work to achieve their goal, their desired end result. Working hard for what you want to achieve is certainly a very worthwhile trait to adopt from the ants. Be diligent in your efforts. As (Proverbs 21:5) puts it, "The plans of the diligent lead to profit as surely as haste leads to poverty."

2. **Goal-oriented**: As soon as one of the ants smells that crumb of food and finds it, he calls for his entourage. They all work together toward a common purpose, getting enough food for the winter. They are goal-oriented and do not give up. It would be as if they have determined the shortest distance between the food and their house, their main goal is to get the food to the storage facility and they are focused on the same end result.

3. **Patience:** It is said that patience is a virtue, and the ants are very patient. If you try to smudge or destroy their line, you will find that after a while they will be come back again to rebuild the path they had before. They can carry their food for hundreds of miles just to get back to their home. It does not matter how long the task will take, they will not disperse until it is done.

4. **Being Consistent**: When I was small, I used to love to watch the ants. Sometimes, I would even drop some food on the ground just to watch them carry it. They surely knew how to find the food; wherever there is food, they will find it. They don't make absences or excuses, they always show up on time, as soon as you are up, they are there already working.

5. **Being Disciplined**: Though they don't have a leader, they are very much disciplined in their work and lifestyle. The ants have

some serious work ethics—they are always on time and they never give up until the task at hand is complete. I think their motto is "always to excel.". Talk about work ethics and you'll see that ants excel in it. They are constantly on the move, working, carrying food from one place to another. No one has to breathe down their backs for them to be busy or look busy.

6. **Be Unified**: Being united with the same goal in mind no doubt creates oneness in motion and purpose. They stay focused on one thing: to gather enough food for all of them to eat during the winter. They unite in their goal; they are all unified reaching their quota of food for all to partake of.

7. **Be Knowledgeable**: The ants are always on the search for food. As they go on their search, they leave a trail of pheromones that helps them find their way back home. As soon as they find some food, they follow their own trail back to the nest and get the help from the colony. They definitely know where to find food. Just drop some sugar, wait for a while, and you'll see an ant… then see how fast their number multiplies moments later. You will see a whole line of ants carrying that lump of sugar to their nest. I would also imagine that they have the strongest sense of smell, which allows them to send their radar out and zero in on the target.

All of these are very valuable traits that we can learn and apply to our lives to achieve more fulfilment. Let us be warned not to give in to laziness. We should be diligent lest we are taken over by poverty. Hard work will return rewards, and our path will eventually be made easier as we reap the rewards of our labor.

Be Diligent in All That You Do

"And whatsoever you do, do it heartily as to the Lord and not unto men knowing that from the Lord you shall receive the reward of the inheritance." (Colossians 3:23-24)

My mother used to say hard work will never kill anyone. Over the past thirty years I have definitely lived this motto: Work as for God and not for man. Over my lifelong careers working for others,

I have developed the habit of working like no other. In 1993 when I told my boss I was thinking of migrating to Canada, he asked me to train someone else to take over my job. He hired a new person whom I trained to take over, but unfortunately, he was not able to take over my entire role. I ended up training three persons to take over what I was doing alone. I thought to myself that since the company had grown so much in sales, since I took over the ordering there was much more stock to account for so then it was normal for the work to be heavier.

A few years later, the same thing happened in a department in which I worked for. I decided to take a temporary position for a year, from the other position I'd held for the past five years, just to learn some new skills. However, as my job was posted and filled, I learned that the newly hired quit after one week, citing that the work was suited for more than one person.

The position was eventually split into four positions, hence four new hires. I therefore made the decision that if I am going to work that hard for someone else, then it is time for me to definitely put some of that energy into something I truly enjoy. Working diligently at what you enjoy and do best, will surely lead you to a life of service before kings, a life that will reap you abundance so you are able to give without sparing.

PRINCIPLE #9

The ninth principle is that of **working hard, but I will encourage you to also work smart**. "All hard work brings a profit, but mere talk leads only to poverty." (Proverbs 14:23) In Proverbs 28:19, it also says, "Those who work their land will have abundant food, but those who chase fantasies will have their fill of poverty."

Scripture talks a lot about working hard with happiness while serving God at your job or workplace. Always work as if you were working for God and not your employer. The Bible and life tells us that hard work will always bring some type of profit. When we think about profit, we usually think about money, but it can be anything. For example, hard work in school will lead to more knowledge, success in your exams, a better job, and more opportunities. Working hard at eliminating your debts and increasing your savings will lead to financial freedom. "Show yourself in all aspect to be a model of good works, and in your teaching, show integrity, dignity, and sound speech that cannot be condemned, so that an opponent may be put to shame, having nothing evil to say about you." (Titus 2:7-8)

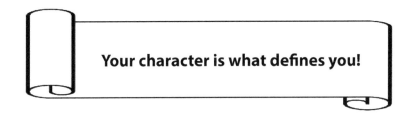

Your character is what defines you!

Building Character

In many areas of our society, it would seem that laziness is rewarded. I have seen many people try to take advantage of the work system, where they work only enough to be eligible for employment insurance benefits. Some even pretend to be ill just to get paid to do nothing. Many are full of excuses for not working. For this they will always be in want and will go hungry. "Laziness brings on deep sleep and the shiftless man goes hungry." (Proverbs 19:15)

One of the purposes of hard work is to build character. A job is not merely designed for us to earn money but should be viewed as a step on the ladder of life or an elevator to help us to our ultimate goal of success. Throughout our life's work, we should use our God-given talents and gifts to build a godly character. "Commit all your work to the Lord and your plans will succeed." (Proverbs 16:3)

(1 Timothy 4:12-14) also says, "Don't let anyone look down on you because you are young, but set an example for the believers in speech, in conduct, in love, in faith and in purity. Until I

come, devote yourself to the public reading of Scripture, to preaching and to teaching. Do not neglect your gift, which was given you through prophecy when the body of elders laid their hands on you." It should not matter how old or young you are, your life should be lived as such that it is an example for others to follow, as they see Christ in you.

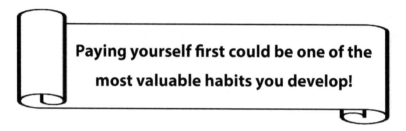

Paying yourself first could be one of the most valuable habits you develop!

With Character Comes Discipline

Though hard work will lead you to create an honest income, you will never find the road to building wealth until you have made the decision that a part of what you earn is yours to keep. If you keep at least ten percent of what you earn, how much would you have accumulated if you did that for ten years? And what if you now put that money to work for you? It often seems that we are more eager to spend what we earn, and in many cases, spend more than what we earn rather than save. We give it to the department store, the cable company, the telephone company, but we never give to ourselves by paying ourselves first. So the first ten percent goes to enhance the work of God, and the next ten percent goes to you. This is the one most valuable habit we can develop.

The four most valuable habits in wealth building are:

1. Give back to enhance the work of God.
2. Pay yourself at least ten percent of what you earn.
3. Live on less than you make.
4. Make your savings work for you.

Don't be that person with big dreams who says I'm going to do this and that, but never do anything. You set goals and have no action to achieve it. Faith without works is dead. Don't be that person who wants the results of labor without sweating. A dream without a goal or an action is definitely a nightmare. Develop the discipline to create a plan of action and stick to it.

"Write down the revelation and make it plain on tablets so that a herald may run with it. For the revelation awaits an appointed time; it speaks of the end and will not prove false. Though it linger, wait for it; it will certainly come and will not delay." (Habakkuk 2:2-3). It is very important to have goals and write them down. One week after I made a decision to put my goals on a dream board, they started to become real. I had on it successful writer, publishing contract, among other things. Within a week of writing them down, I met Kary Oberbrunner who has been very instrumental in helping me achieve my goal as a successful writer, and here I am just over six months later, publishing my first book. Dreams do come true so I encourage you to take action today!

Working Smart

Some people will encourage you to work smart and not hard. But I will encourage you to do both. Whatever you do, do it heartily as for the Lord and not for men. (Colossians 3:23) From the words of the bible we are encouraged not only to work hard, but also to be wise in our doings. If you are physically, mentally, and emotionally able to work, you should do so and to the best of your ability. No matter how menial the task at hand may seem, you should do it with zest and zeal. We should also be wise to incorporate godly work ethics in whatever we do. We should shrug off laziness and give glory to God in all aspects of our work. Working united in a team will also offer many more benefits as you can achieve much more than doing it alone. When there is unity in diversity, then the ordinary person can do extraordinary things. "Just as a body, though one, has many parts, but all its many parts form one body, so it is with Christ… Even so, the body is not made up of one part but of many." (1Corinthians 12:12 &14)

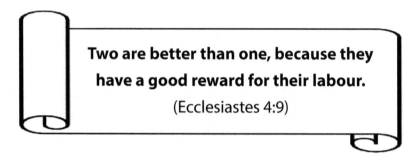

Two are better than one, because they have a good reward for their labour.
(Ecclesiastes 4:9)

In the book of Ecclesiastes, in chapter 4, much wisdom is found within that encourages team work—two are better than one because they have a good reward for their labor. There are many advantages of working together with others. Each one will come with different talents and skills, and together can become a power house. Life is designed for companionship and not isolation, as we are here to serve God and our fellow man.

It is said that there are many ways to build wealth, but I will implore that there are two sure ways to maximize your efforts and build wealth. You can either:

1. Have a lot of money to put to work for you, or

2. Have a lot of people working with you.

Bearing in mind the statistics that 95 percent of people will retire at or below the poverty line, and will not be able to afford the basic necessities of living during retirement, it has become obvious that most people do not have a lot of money to work for them.

It would therefore be in the best interest of many to use the latter to gain the former. (*Have a team of people working with you to achieve the financial goals you have set, then put that money to work for you.*) Two are better than one, because they have a good reward for their toil. For if one falls, the other will lift up his fellow. But woe to him who is alone when he falls and has not another to lift him up! Again, if two lie together, they keep warm, but how can one keep warm alone? And though a man might prevail against one who is alone, two will withstand him—a threefold cord is not quickly broken.

The Essentials of Teamwork

According to (Proverbs 27:17), "iron sharpens iron, so a man sharpens the countenance of his friend." It is amazing to know how much we feed off the energy of each other. When you surround yourself with positive, vibrant, energetic, and enthusiastic individuals, you will be amazed at what you can produce. Not only should you have a team, but your team should be in one accord, having similar goals and vision. "Then make my joy complete by being like-minded, having the same love, being one in spirit and of one mind." (Philippians 2:2) *Being in one* accord, of one mind, suggests a team working towards the same common goal. Team unity is an essential component in having success in anything you do. Teamwork is dream work, as more can be accomplished by working together toward fulfilling a mission.

Laziness Breeds Contempt

God looks down on laziness, but he shows that with hard work you can accomplish many things in life. When you're in God's will, He will strengthen you daily and help you to achieve success. "The soul of the sluggard craves and gets nothing, while the soul of the diligent is richly supplied." (Proverbs 13:4) "A slack hand causes poverty, but the hand of the diligent makes rich." (Proverbs 10:4) "I went past the field of a sluggard, past the vineyard of someone who has no sense; thorns had come up everywhere, the ground was covered with weeds, and the stone wall was in ruins. I applied my heart to what I observed and learned a lesson from what I saw: A little sleep, a little slumber, a little folding of the hands to rest—and poverty will come on you like a thief and scarcity like an armed man." (Proverbs 24:30-34) "But if anyone does not provide for his relatives, and especially for members of his household, he has denied the faith and is worse than an unbeliever." (1 Timothy 5:8)

It is very important for one to provide for their family as this is a way to honor God. Neglecting your responsibilities to your family is denying your faith in the master.

Whatever you do, work at it with all your heart, as working for the Lord, not for human masters. If you make it a habit to do this in all you do, it will truly make a huge difference in your outcome.

Action Step #9

Starting today: When you work, do your work as you are working for God and not for man. Whatever you do, work at it with all your heart, as working for the Lord, not for human masters.

(Colossians 3:23)

10

SEEK GODLY COUNSEL

I met Matthew while canvassing in the community one bright Saturday afternoon. We often go out just to meet folks and do surveys to see how best we can meet the needs of people in the community. He was a very jovial character. We met a few times at the local snack shop where we would share information and spend some time talking about different topics in the bible and other things that would normally affect our lives. Matthew told me the story of his adventure when he left his home country, and his quest for finding a way to build a fortune.

Matthew said, "My dad always told me to 'never put your eggs in one basket.' However, I have been searching for the right place to put my eggs without any success."

"Where have you looked?" I asked.

"Oh, here and there," he said. "I once gave a friend of mine a large sum to invest. He totally convinced me that a so-called ship would get me emeralds and I would double my money in ten days. I totally believed him. The only thing is, the ship never reached shore. A few of the members were arrested. I never saw my money again."

"What did your friend do for a living?" I asked. "He was a construction worker, not sure why I chose to trust a construction worker with my investment. I certainly did learn the hard way." "Would you go to a shoemaker to buy a loaf of bread? Or a shop-keeper to buy a car?" I asked. "Of course not," he said. "So why did you trust a construction worker with your investment?"

Many persons are tempted to put their hard earned money into things that promise quick riches. It is better to seek counsel from those who have experience handling money through proper investing than to trust a broke friend who is merely going by a hunch. It is therefore wise to seek godly counsel before investing. Good, sound, and godly financial advice can be had with no additional charge to you.

PRINCIPLE #10

Principle number ten is that of **seeking godly counsel**. In (Psalm 1:1), the word declares, "Blessed is the one who does not walk in step with the wicked or stand in the way that sinners take or sit in the company of mockers." A person needing financial advice should not go to someone who makes his living selling the very thing he's contemplating buying. You should also seek financial advice from someone who follows similar moral principles that you believe in. "Plans fail for lack of counsel, but with many advisers they succeed." (Proverbs 15:22). Before buying a house, purchasing a car, or even borrowing money, pray about it and seek the counsel of godly advisors. They can steer you from making a lot of mistakes. One of the reasons many do not seek counsel is that they don't want to be told by someone else that an intended action is unsound; they just like to do what they want anyway.

We need to put pride aside and seek the proper counsel we need.

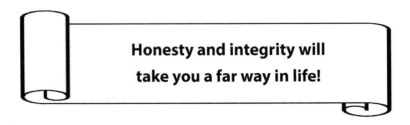

Honesty and integrity will take you a far way in life!

The Truth Will Find You Out

One of the most successful ploys of the devil is to keep you in poverty. I could actually say his plan has been successful in that over ninety-five percent (95%) of people in the world are living at or below the poverty line. This result is due to the fact that people are not walking in the way that they should. They are not honoring God and trusting him in all things. God's promises are sure, he never lies. As each of us are created with a measure of faith, we ought to exercise that faith. In (Malachi 3: 6-7), it states: "I the LORD DOES NOT CHANGE. So you, the descendants of Jacob, are not destroyed. Ever since the time of your ancestors you have turned away from my decrees and have not kept them. Return to me, and I will return to you," says the Lord Almighty." (James 1:5) also advises, "If any of you lacks wisdom, you should ask God, who gives generously to all without finding fault, and it will be given to you."

Throughout your lifetime, it is very likely that your desires will become greater than you can gratify. Unfortunately, many will yield to these desires without the proper means to acquire them. This is surely what leads to acquisition of massive debt, and eventually, poverty. The devil is a coward and hits you at your weakest point. Take heart, however, that this can be reversed. (Ephesians 4: 17-24) states: "So I tell you this, and insist on it in the Lord, that you must no longer live as the Gentiles do, in the futility of their thinking. They are darkened in their understanding and separated from the life of God because of the ignorance that is in them due to the hardening of their hearts. Having lost all sensitivity, they have given themselves over to sensuality so as to indulge in every kind of impurity, and they are full of greed." That, however, is not the way of life you learned when you heard about Christ and were taught that in him we should live in accordance with the truth that is found in Jesus. You were taught, with regard to your former way of life, to put off your old self, which is being corrupted by its deceitful desires; to be made new in the attitude of your minds; and to put on the new self, created to be with godly character, in true righteousness and holiness. God is watching you in everything you do, so why not put on a grand show?

Clarify Your Intentions

You have to be intentional about changing your life, and changing your family's legacy to a generation of wealth builders. Generational wealth is biblical, as written in (Proverbs 13:22), "A good man leaves an inheritance to his children's children, and the wealth of the sinner is stored up for the righteous." If we teach our children proper spiritual stewardship, and they pass it on to their children, there will be a positive change in our family's legacy for generations to come. "Whoever walks in integrity will be delivered, but he who is crooked in his ways will suddenly fall." (Proverbs 28:18) Be clear in your intentions, and be careful not to give mixed signals. Clear communication is an integral part of giving clarity to your intentions.

Honesty is the best policy, and the first person you need to be honest with is yourself. Be transparent in whatever you do. Say what you mean and mean what you say. Make sure your communication to those you are working with is very clear in order for your team to be in line with your goals. This will get you the best results.

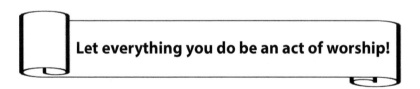

Let everything you do be an act of worship!

You should endeavour to get rid of any desires that are not in harmony with your greater spiritual goals. "For now we see in a mirror dimly, but then face to face; now I know in part, but then I will know fully just as I also have been fully known." (1 Corinthian 13:12) Through Paul's eyes, we are offered a glimpse of what the future may be so we may have hope. Sometimes you will find it hard to let go of the things that are holding you back but you must free yourself of those baggage in order to move forward. Let go of the things and individuals in your life that are hindrances to your progress.

Constantly seek communion with God for him to show you what your gifts are, and use them to your best ability. Wisdom comes from God, so seek him continually. Ask for divine fulfillment and a deeper meaning to life. Be open minded, and accept the inevitable, as things will not always go as you plan. Also, do not expect things to be what they are not. Call a spade a spade. Honesty and integrity will take you a far way in life. Let everything you do be an act of worship to God that others may see your works and be drawn closer to Him.

The Two Evils

It is very important to avoid the following two evils:

1. The spirit of poverty: The devil uses this is a ploy to enslave us into thinking that money is bad. Money is merely a medium of exchange that will enable us to do things to enhance God's kingdom. It is not money that is bad but, as explained in 1 Timothy 6:10, "the love of money is the root of all evil." We should therefore not give in to the spirit of poverty, as this is where the feeling of envy is rooted. Envy thinks that if we cannot get what others have, then they should not have it either. These thoughts are unbiblical, and we should not give in to these temptations.

2. The spirit of pride: We should recognize that wealth does not come from our hard work alone. Every good and perfect gift comes from above. If you who are evil know how to give good gifts to your children, how much more would your heavenly father and Creator know what gifts are best suited for you? Remember, all wealth comes from God as he sees fit to bestow his grace upon you. "We have heard of the pride of Moab—how proud he is! —Of his arrogance, his pride, and his insolence; in his idle boasting he is not right." (Isaiah 16:6)

"Humble yourselves therefore before the Lord and he will lift you up." (James 4:10). "For the reward of humility is fear of the Lord in riches and honor and life everlasting." (Proverbs 22:4)

Defeating the Two Evils

It is imperative that we live our functioning lives on gratitude and humility. Everything we do should be an act of worship. When we live with the spirit of gratitude towards God and others whom he has placed in our path of life, we are practicing biblical steward-ship. We are managers of what God has entrusted us with, and not owners. Stay away from the bingo barn and the race track. Nothing is by chance. Hard work and a strategic plan will get you to a comfortable place financially. If you fail to plan, you are definitely planning to fail. "Be thou diligent to know the state of thy flocks, and look well into thy herds." (Proverbs 27: 23)

You should know your financial condition. "Now therefore consider your ways, you have sown much, but harvest little; you eat, but there is not enough to be satisfied; you drink, but there is not enough to become drunk; you put on clothing, but no one is warm enough; and he who earns, earns wages to put into a purse with holes. Consider your ways, says the Lord. Think carefully about what you are doing. For the wages of sin is death, and the gift of God is eternal life in Christ Jesus."(Romans 6:22)

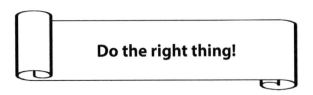

Do the right thing!

Learn to Read the Fine Print

Many of us are guilty of signing documents before we read the fine print, and we certainly pay for it later when things don't go the way we perceive. Above all, don't sign anything until you check the deal thoroughly first. Don't be hurried into any deals. The worst deal in the world is often the one in which a person is rushed into signing, capitulating to a relentless salesman's chance-of-a-lifetime-offer pressure tactics. The best offer in the world can wait. Go with your gut feeling, and with God's guidance you will end up doing the right thing.

Leaving a Legacy

Morris was a man who was not afraid of hard work. He was, however, one who loved flashy things. He told me he had to have a new car every three years, which he normally leases from the dealership. He wore really nice and expensive clothes and he also travelled a lot. Sometimes I wonder if he thinks he would be able to work forever. One day I mentioned to him the possibility of leaving a legacy to his children, just in case. He never gave a second thought to the fact that the lifestyle he was leading would contribute to his demise.

After a few years, he developed diabetes. When he began to think about what may eventually happen to him, it was too late and he had developed so many illnesses that he had now become uninsurable. As the money dwindled and the flashy cars disappeared, so did his so-called friends. He had only a handful of people who really stood by him. Every day he would reminisce on what his life used to be. You see, he did not make provisions for tomorrow, he lived only for today. When it was time for him to be buried, the family had to ask for help from people in the community. This was a very sad time for his family.

As I sit with people from all walks of life, my main goal is to educate them on what the possibilities are in sharing various scenarios that I have witnessed. It is very important to make provisions for your family by building a solid financial foundation that your family will not be in want, should you not be around to provide for them. It is very easy to have some protection when you are younger, and this will ease the burden of your family in the long run. This protection can be made by making small payments at regular intervals. This could serve to provide a good sum to help your family if you are not around. Therefore, be wise and build a solid foundation.

"Be thou diligent to know the state of thy flocks and look well to thy herds. For riches are not forever; and doth the crown endure to generation?" (Proverbs 27:23-24) Know well your financial condition and make preparations for the future. Would you start building a house from the roof? Any good builder would start with a solid foundation. Then they can be sure the house will be sturdy and is able to withstand the storms.

Your financial house is no different, so start building from the foundation. You are the most valuable asset, as the breadwinner of your family. You should secure your ability to earn, so there will always be food in your house. God wants us to obtain counsel as noted in (Proverbs 15:22): "Plans fail for lack of counsel, but with many advisers they succeed." First, you should spend quality time with the Lord in prayer and seek his guidance in all areas of your life. Let God's word guide you to make proper and sound financial decisions. Do not go into debt, and if you have to, make it minimal, with a plan to pay it off as quickly as possible.

It may take the advice of two or even three godly counsellors to help you make big financial decisions. This should be people who are firmly grounded in God's word and understand and apply the knowledge. If you have a spouse, make sure he or she is part of the decision-making process. Proceed only after you have a clear indication that this is the direction God wants you to take.

As I had suggested in Action Step #4, I encourage you to find a financial advisor and request a Financial Needs Analysis (FNA) in order to determine your state of affairs, and create a plan to help you realize your goals. You will definitely need a financial diagnosis in order to find the right remedy for your situation.

Action Step #10

Now that you have completed your FNA (Financial Needs Analysis), it is time to work on a step by step plan with your financial advisor to create solutions tailored to your unique situation.

Build a solid financial foundation. It is not about you, it is about God and your family.

THE RECIPE

You have just uncovered ten biblical principles that can change your life. However, change can only come about if we take action, as faith without works is dead. Every action begins with a thought. Thought plus belief or faith plus action equals results. The persistence of repetitive actions in the right direction will lead to success.

"What good is it, my brothers, if someone says he has faith but does not have works? Can that faith save him? If a brother or sister is poorly clothed and lacking in daily food, and one of you says to them, 'Go in peace, be warmed and filled,' without giving them the things needed for the body, what good is that? So also faith by itself, if it does not have works, is dead." (James 2: 14-17) "For if anyone is a hearer of the word and not a doer, he is like a man who looks intently at his natural face in a mirror. For he looks at himself and goes away and at once forgets what he was like. But the one who looks into the perfect law, the law of liberty, and perseveres, being no hearer who forgets but a doer who acts, he will be blessed in his doings". (James 1: 23-25) God is working on changing the person in your mirror. He wants you to be a better person, he wants you to win as you have never won before. You just need to have a plan and stick to it and trust in Him. No one said it was going to be easy, but you have to make a decision and start something now. God has a game plan that works every time; of course there are going to be some obstacles and a few bumps in the road. "Not by might or by power, but by the Spirit," says the Lord. He has a plan for your life so you should "seek first the kingdom of God and his righteousness and all other things will be given to you." (Zechariah 4:6)

In Summary

These are the TEN biblical financial principles to live by:

- God is the source
- Keep out of debt
- Live on the margins of life
- Save and invest
- Giving is essential
- Be content with what you have
- Keep records and have a budget
- Don't co-sign
- Work hard and work smart
- Seek godly counsel.

The truth is, we tend to hold on to what we think is more valuable to us. Unfortunately, because money is a tangible resource, we tend to put more value to it than we really should. As you learn to follow these eternal principles in your personal finances and in other areas of your life, you will know the joy that comes from trusting and obeying God in all areas of your life.

We should remember that God wants us to be good stewards of the resources he gives us. He gives us gifts in order to build us up, to strengthen, help, and encourage others. These gifts are to be used to honor and glorify God while we are here on earth. It is in true obedience to Him that we will be lead to eternal prosperity.

Prayer

Father, you have given me knowledge, please teach me now how to use it wisely. Father, help me to find a way somehow to help make this world a better place. I thank you for your grace and your mercy. You have promised that goodness and mercy shall follow me all the days of my life. Help me to live in true obedience to you.

Father, put purpose in my days, so that all my talents, my education, and my skills, may find true fulfillment as I learn to do your will. May my life be aligned with your will, so my true purpose will be achieved.

Lord, may you command your blessings on my finances today. I give all my worries and fear regarding my finances over to you. Thank you for giving me the will to live within my means, save and invest, and the obedience to give back to you, the first fruits of all my increase. I pray that the Holy Spirit will continually dwell within me to teach me your way of righteousness, and help me to recognize the opportunities that are meant to be a blessing to me and to those whom you have placed at different points in my journey. I thank you for everything.

Amen.

BIBLIOGRAPHY

The Holy Bible   *King James Versions*

Bible Gateway   *New International Version*

The Storehouse Principle: *Al Jaindl and Van Crouch*

Total Money Makeover: *Dave Ramsay*

Saving Your Future *Xuan Nguyen*

The Science of Getting Rich *Wallace D. Wattles*

The Speed of Trust *Stephen Covey*

Acknowledgements

First and foremost, I give thanks to God Almighty for his inspiration and loving kindness in providing the means and contents of this book.

Special thanks to Kary Oberbrunner and his team for gracefully allowing me the opportunity to work alongside them with this project.

To Sam and Maria Lawal for encouraging me to pursue my dream.

Cetalyn McNeish who, through her faith, strength, and prayers, helped and encouraged me in times when I felt like I could not go on, and adding her touch as a literary scholar, to you I am very grateful.

To all who will read this book, I thank you for your support, and I pray that you will be lead to take action buy moving from thinking to doing.

APPENDIX A

Reflections

For if anyone is a hearer of the word and not a doer, he is like a man who looks intently at his natural face in a mirror. For he looks at himself and goes away and at once forgets what he was like. But the one who looks into the perfect law, the law of liberty, and perseveres, being no hearer who forgets but a doer who acts, he will be blessed in his doing. (James 1:23-25)

As for the rich in this present age, charge them not to be haughty, nor to set their hopes on the uncertainty of riches, but on God, who richly provides us with everything to enjoy. They are to do good, to be rich in good works, to be generous and ready to share, thus storing up treasure for themselves as a good foundation for the future, so that they may take hold of that which is truly life. (1 Timothy 6:17-19)

APPENDIX B

Simple Budget Worksheet

Monthly Expenses	Actual Amt.	Income	Percentage	New Amt.
Tithe			10%	
Savings			10%	
			80%	
Mortgage/Rent				
Utilities (light, heat, sewer)				
Child Care				
Food				
Auto Loan				
Credit Card				
Personal Loan				
Other				
Total				

APPENDIX C

SOME FOOD FOR THOUGHT

- Did you know that over 3 billion people, that is about half the world's population, live on less than $2.50 a day, and 80% of humanity lives on less than $10 a day? *(Saving Your Future-Xuan Nguyen)*

- There are many who are homeless, even though they are employed.

- Many families are only one paycheck away from becoming homeless. As a matter of fact, more than forty percent of the world's homeless have a job and cannot afford to live in a home.

- There is enough wealth in the world to feed, clothe, and shelter every human being on the planet, and provide them with a comfortable living, yet more and more individuals are ending up on the streets or dying of hunger.

- Our churches are poor because we are poor, or should we say, our priorities are not in obedience with God's principles.

- Our obedience to God has a direct correlation to our ultimate financial health.

ABOUT THE AUTHOR

Delores Hamilton-McKenzie was born in St. Catherine, Jamaica to Alfred and Dorothy Coombs-Hamilton. She had a wonderful and happy childhood in a family where free expression and creativity were encouraged. Her father was a building contractor and carpenter, and her mother was an entrepreneur. Delores recalls an early childhood filled with a life of abundance and plenty of food. There was always enough for anyone who passed by. Her mother was always helping others to make a better life for themselves.

The principles of charity, joy, peace, patience, kindness, goodness, generosity, gentleness, faithfulness, modesty, self-control, contentment, and finding value in everything were instilled in her by her parents. Throughout her life, Delores has seen many families and individuals suffer due to lack of knowledge. These experiences have ignited a passion in Delores to help keep her family's legacy alive by helping others become financially independent through the application of godly principles.

Delores was educated at St. Mary's College in Above Rocks, St. Catherine, and Duffs Business College in Kingston, Jamaica where she did Business Management and Accounting. She moved to Canada in 1993 to accept a job offer. She maintained that job for three years, then transitioned into health care where she has served for the past 16 years. Delores is a Licensed Financial Educator and is licensed with The Alberta Insurance Council. She is currently building her financial services business in one of the fastest growing companies in North America that is revolutionizing the financial industry.

She is the author of *The Heart of Obedience: 10 Biblical Financial Principles to Change Your Life,* with many more books to come. Delores loves travelling the world and meeting new people. Her goal is to inspire you to rise above your circumstances by opening your mind to envision the promises of the Creator and become financially independent to live a life of abundance! Her motto can be found in Philippians 4:13: "I can do all things through Christ who strengthens me."

Delores is married to Liston McKenzie and they have three children and three grandchildren.

Thought: 1 Timothy 6:17-19

As for the rich in this present age, charge them not to be haughty, nor to set their hopes on the uncertainty of riches, but on God, who richly provides us with everything to enjoy. They are to do good, to be rich in good works, to be generous and ready to share, thus storing up treasure for themselves as a good foundation for the future, so that they may take hold of that which is truly life.

Contact: theartofobedience@gmail.com

Connect:

http://www.theartofobedience.com/

theartofobedience@gmail.com

These 10 Biblical principles will help you eliminate your debt and start the road to a solid financial foundation

WE DO SMALL AND LARGE GROUP WORKSHOPS

10 Biblical Financial Principles Workbook

Moving from thinking to doing!

OUR TEAM HAS HELPED HUNDREDS OF PEOPLE BUILD THEIR SOLID FINANCIAL FOUNDATION

Cell: 403-836-3343

Delores McKenzie
403-836-3343
mckenzie.delores@gmail.com

theartofobedience
@gmail.com